The Wiersbe BIBLE STUDY SERIES

I KINGS

The Wiersbe BIBLE STUDY SERIES

Being Good Stewards of God's Gifts

THE WIERSBE BIBLE STUDY SERIES: 1 KINGS
Published by David C Cook
4050 Lee Vance View
Colorado Springs, CO 80918 U.S.A.

David C Cook Distribution Canada
55 Woodslee Avenue, Paris, Ontario, Canada N3L 3E5

David C Cook U.K., Kingsway Communications
Eastbourne, East Sussex BN23 6NT, England

The graphic circle C logo is a registered trademark of David C Cook.

ISBN 978-1-4347-0697-3
eISBN 978-1-4347-0959-2

The Team: Steve Parolini, Karen Lee-Thorp, Amy Konyndyk,
Nick Lee, Jack Campbell, Channing Brooks, Karen Athen
Series Cover Design: John Hamilton Design
Cover Photo: iStockphoto

Printed in the United States of America
First Edition 2015

1 2 3 4 5 6 7 8 9 10

082815

Contents

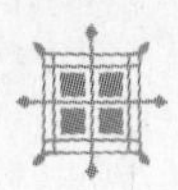

Introduction to 1 Kings

The Blame Game

An ancient proverb says, "A bad workman always blames his tools."

William Bennett, a contemporary writer, said, "Responsible persons are mature people who have taken charge of themselves and their conduct, who own their actions and *own up* to them—who *answer* for them."

Finding someone else to blame, denying responsibility, and hiding behind lies seem to be the order of the day. A comedian gets laughs when he says, "The devil made me do it." In contrast, President Harry Truman had a sign on his desk that said, "The buck stops here." He wasn't afraid to take responsibility. "If you can't stand the heat," he said, "get out of the kitchen!"

David knew what it meant to be a responsible leader, and so did his son Solomon, until the closing years of his reign.

Responsibility

After Solomon's death, the nation divided into the ten tribes of the northern kingdom of Israel and the two tribes of Judah. Following Solomon, only eight could be called good kings and responsible men who sought to obey God. For the sake of David, the Lord kept the light shining in Jerusalem and a king on the throne of Judah until the nation was taken captive by Babylon.

But it wasn't only a dozen kings whose irresponsibility brought about the destruction of the city and temple and the captivity of the people. The prophet Jeremiah reminds us that "the sins of her prophets and the iniquities of her priests" also contributed to Israel's downfall (Lam. 4:13). Prophets, priests, and kings were God's chosen and anointed leaders for His people; yet during the 450 years of Jewish national history before the fall of Jerusalem, most of the prophets and priests failed both God and the people.

Integrity is one of the vital foundations of society, but integrity involves taking responsibility and facing accountability. This includes leadership in the home and church as well as in the halls of academe and the political chambers. It's one thing to make promises at the church altar or to take an oath of office, but it's quite another to assume responsibility and act with courage and honesty and seek to please God.

—Warren W. Wiersbe

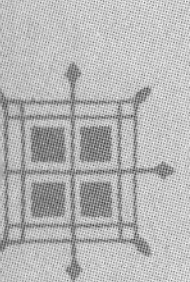

How to Use This Study

This study is designed for both individual and small-group use. We've divided it into eight lessons—each references one or more chapters in Warren W. Wiersbe's commentary *Be Responsible* (second edition, David C Cook, 2010). While reading *Be Responsible* is not a prerequisite for going through this study, the additional insights and background Wiersbe offers can greatly enhance your study experience.

The **Getting Started** questions at the beginning of each lesson offer you an opportunity to record your first thoughts and reactions to the study text. This is an important step in the study process as those "first impressions" often include clues about what it is your heart is longing to discover.

The bulk of the study is found in the **Going Deeper** questions. These dive into the Bible text and, along with helpful excerpts from Wiersbe's commentary, help you examine not only the original context and meaning of the verses but also modern application.

Looking Inward narrows the focus down to your personal story. These intimate questions can be a bit uncomfortable at times, but don't shy away from honesty here. This is where you are asked to stand before the mirror of God's Word and look closely at what you see. It's the place to take a good look at yourself in light of the lesson and search for ways in which you can grow in faith.

Going Forward is the place where you can commit to paper those things you want or need to do in order to better live out the discoveries you made in the Looking Inward section. Don't skip or skim through this. Take the time to really consider what practical steps you might take to move closer to Christ. Then share your thoughts with a trusted friend who can act as an encourager and accountability partner.

Finally, there is a brief **Seeking Help** section to close the lesson. This is a reminder for you to invite God into your spiritual-growth process. If you choose to write out a prayer in this section, come back to it as you work through the lesson and continue to seek the Holy Spirit's guidance as you discover God's will for your life.

Tips for Small Groups

A small group is a dynamic thing. One week it might seem like a group of close-knit friends. The next it might seem more like a group of uncomfortable strangers. A small-group leader's role is to read these subtle changes and adjust the tone of the discussion accordingly.

Small groups need to be safe places for people to talk openly. It is through shared wrestling with difficult life issues that some of the greatest personal growth is discovered. But in order for the group to feel safe, participants need to know it's okay *not* to share sometimes. Always invite honest disclosure, but never force someone to speak if he or she isn't comfortable doing so. (A savvy leader will follow up later with a group member who isn't comfortable sharing in a group setting to see if a one-on-one discussion is more appropriate.)

Have volunteers take turns reading excerpts from Scripture or from the commentary. The more each person is involved even in the mundane tasks, the more he or she will feel comfortable opening up in more meaningful ways.

The leader should watch the clock and keep the discussion moving. Sometimes there may be more Going Deeper questions than your group can cover in your available time. If you've had a fruitful discussion, it's okay to move on without finishing everything. And if you think the group is getting bogged down on a question or has taken off on a tangent, you can simply say, "Let's go on to question 5." Be sure to save at least ten to fifteen minutes for the Going Forward questions.

Finally, soak your group meetings in prayer—before you begin, during as needed, and always at the end of your time together.

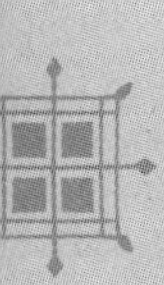

Wisdom

(1 KINGS 1—4; 1 CHRONICLES 29:22–30; 2 CHRONICLES 1)

Before you begin ...

- *Pray for the Holy Spirit to reveal truth and wisdom as you go through this lesson.*
- *Read 1 Kings 1—4; 1 Chronicles 29:22–30; and 2 Chronicles 1. This lesson references chapters 1 and 2 in* Be Responsible. *It will be helpful for you to have your Bible and a copy of the commentary available as you work through this lesson.*

Getting Started

From the Commentary

The kingdom of Israel was facing a crisis because King David was on his deathbed. In facing this crisis, different people responded in different ways.

A real leader looks at a crisis and asks, "What can I do that will best help the people?" An opportunist looks at a crisis and asks, "How can I use this situation to promote

> myself and get what I want?" Opportunists usually show up uninvited, focus attention on themselves, and end up making the crisis worse. Adonijah was that kind of person.
>
> Adonijah was David's oldest living son and was probably thirty-five years old at this time. David's firstborn, Amnon, was killed by Absalom; his second son, Kileab (or Daniel), must have died young because there's no record of his life; and the third son, Absalom, was slain by Joab (1 Chron. 3:1–2). As David's eldest son, Adonijah felt that he deserved the throne. After all, his father was a sick man who would soon die, and it was important that there be a king on the throne of Israel. Like his older brother Absalom (2 Sam. 15:1–6), Adonijah seized his opportunity when David wasn't at his best and was bedfast.
>
> —*Be Responsible*, pages 15–16

1. Review 1 Kings 1:1–10. In what ways was Adonijah an opportunist? In what ways did Adonijah underestimate David? What are some ways people are similarly opportunistic in today's church? Why is it tempting to take advantage of people whose power or influence seems to be waning?

More to Consider: Following the example of his infamous brother Absalom (2 Sam. 15:1–12), Adonijah began to promote himself and generate popular support. Like Absalom, he was a handsome man who had been pampered by his father (1 Kings 1:6; 2 Sam. 13—14), and the unthinking people joined his crusade. How might the way his father had pampered him have contributed to his decision to take over the throne? What does this story reveal to us about the risks of spoiling our children?

2. Choose one verse or phrase from 1 Kings 1—4; 1 Chronicles 29:22–30; or 2 Chronicles 1 that stands out to you. This could be something you're intrigued by, something that makes you uncomfortable, something that puzzles you, something that resonates with you, or just something you want to examine further. Write that here.

Going Deeper

From the Commentary

If ever King David had a loyal friend and adviser, it was the prophet Nathan. Nathan brought the good news about God's covenant with David and his descendants (2 Sam. 7:1–17), and Nathan also shepherded David

> through those dark days after the king's adultery with Bathsheba (2 Sam. 12). Nathan must have had musical gifts as well because he helped David organize the worship in the sanctuary (2 Chron. 29:25–26). When Solomon was born, Nathan told the parents that the Lord wanted the boy also named "Jedidiah—beloved of the Lord" (2 Sam. 12:24–25). When Nathan heard about Adonijah's feast and his claim to the throne, he immediately went to work.
>
> —*Be Responsible*, pages 17–18

3. What did Nathan do when he heard about Adonijah's plans? Why did he go to Bathsheba first? What did he say to David? How did David respond? What does Nathan's role reveal about the importance of having loyal friends?

From the Commentary

> David "served his own generation by the will of God" (Acts 13:36 NKJV), but he was also concerned about Solomon and the next generation. David had his enemies,

some of whom were in his own household and inner circle, and he wanted to be certain that the new king didn't inherit old problems. During his long reign of forty years, David had unified the nation, defeated their enemies, successfully organized kingdom affairs, and made more than adequate preparation for the building of the temple. He sang his last song (2 Sam. 23:1–7) and then gave his last charge to Solomon.

—*Be Responsible*, page 22

4. In what ways was David concerned about the next generation? What does his concern teach us about the roles of leaders in passing the torch to those who follow? What was David's last charge to Solomon? How does this apply to church leaders today?

From the Commentary

The Old Testament records the last words of Jacob (Gen. 49), Moses (Deut. 33), Joshua (Josh. 23:1—24:27), and David (1 Kings 2:1–11). "I am going the way of all the earth" is a quotation from Joshua at the end of his life

> (Josh. 23:14), and "Be strong and show yourself a man" sounds like the Lord's words to Joshua at the start of his ministry (Josh. 1:6). Solomon was a young man who had lived a sheltered life, so he needed this admonition. In fact, from the very outset of his reign, he would have to make some tough decisions and issue some difficult orders. David had already commissioned Solomon regarding building the temple (1 Chron. 22:6–13), a task that would take seven years. One day Solomon would come to the end of his life, and David wanted him to be able to look back with satisfaction. Blessed is that person whose heart is right with God, whose conscience is clear and who can look back and say to the Master: "I have glorified You on the earth. I have finished the work which You have given Me to do" (John 17:4 NKJV)....
>
> The king was expected to be familiar with the law and the covenant (Deut. 17:14–20), for in obeying God's Word he would find his wisdom, strength, and blessing.
>
> —*Be Responsible*, pages 22–23

5. How do David's words to Solomon (1 Kings 2:1–9) echo those of Moses when he commissioned Joshua (Deut. 31:1–8)? What are the differences? Why is the statement "show yourself a man" (1 Kings 2:2) significant in this context? How would that be translated in today's terms?

From the Commentary

The new king had his agenda all prepared: deal with Joab, deal with Shimei, reward the sons of Barzillai, and build the temple. But his first major crisis came from his half brother Adonijah.

Solomon had graciously accepted Adonijah's submission to the new regime (1 Kings 1:53), although Solomon certainly knew that the man was deceitful and ready to strike again. The fact that Adonijah went to the queen mother with his request suggests that he expected her to have great influence with her son.…

Students differ in their interpretation of Bathsheba's role in this scenario. Some say she was very naive in even asking Solomon, but Bathsheba had already proved herself to be a courageous and influential woman. It's likely that she suspected another plot because she knew that possession of a king's wife or concubine was evidence of possession of the kingdom. This was why Absalom had publicly taken David's concubines (2 Sam. 16:20–23), for it was an announcement to the people that he was now king. It's difficult to believe that the king's mother was ignorant of this fact. I may be in error, but I feel that she took Adonijah at his word, *knowing that Solomon would use this as an opportunity to expose Adonijah's scheme.* By having Abishag as his wife, Adonijah was claiming to be coregent with Solomon!

—*Be Responsible*, page 25

6. Review 1 Kings 2:12–46. How does Adonijah's declaration in verse 15 show how confused he was in his thinking? If Solomon was God's choice for the throne, and Adonijah knew it, why did he still attempt a coup? What did this say about his character? What was Solomon's answer to Adonijah's attempt to claim the throne?

From the Commentary

> When Solomon ascended the throne, the people of Israel soon learned that he was not another David. He was a scholar, not a soldier, a man more interested in erecting buildings than fighting battles. David enjoyed the simple life of a shepherd, but Solomon chose to live in luxury. Both David and Solomon wrote songs, but Solomon is better known for his proverbs. We have many of David's songs in the book of Psalms, but except for Psalms 72 and 127, and the Song of Solomon, we have none of Solomon's three thousand songs.
>
> David was a shepherd who loved and served God's flock, while Solomon became a celebrity who used the people to help support his extravagant lifestyle. When David died, the people mourned; after Solomon died, the

> people begged his successor, King Rehoboam, to lighten the heavy yoke his father had put on their necks. David was a warrior who put his trust in God; Solomon was a politician who put his trust in authority, treaties, and achievement.
>
> —*Be Responsible*, page 31

7. What does the contrast between David and Solomon reveal to us about the kinds of leaders God chooses for His people? Solomon is mentioned nearly three hundred times in the Old Testament and a dozen times in the New Testament. What made him such a notable figure in the history of God's people? How is his legacy different from that of his father?

From the Commentary

> Solomon's name comes from the Hebrew word *shalom*, which means "peace," and during his reign, the kingdom was at peace with its neighbors. His father, David, had risked his life on the battlefield to defeat enemy nations and claim their lands for Israel, but Solomon took a different approach to international diplomacy. He made

> treaties with other rulers by marrying their daughters, which helps to explain why he had seven hundred wives who were princesses, as well as three hundred concubines (1 Kings 11:3). It appears that Solomon entered into treaty arrangements with every petty ruler who had a marriageable daughter!…
>
> His first bride after he became king was the daughter of the pharaoh of Egypt, Israel's old enemy. This alliance indicates that Egypt had slipped much lower on the international scene and that Israel was now much higher, because Egyptian rulers didn't give their daughters in marriage to the rulers of other nations. It's significant that Solomon didn't put his Egyptian wife into the royal palace where David had lived, because it was near the ark of the covenant (2 Chron. 8:11), but housed her in another place until her own palace was completed. He spent seven years building the temple of God but thirteen years building his own palace (1 Kings 6:37—7:1).
>
> —*Be Responsible*, pages 32–33

8. How did Solomon's system of treaties cut at the heart of Israel's unique role as God's people? How does Moses' warning to the Jewish kings in Deuteronomy 17:14–20 speak to the choices Solomon made?

More to Consider: The Lord placed Israel among the Gentile nations to be a witness to them of the true and living God, a "light for the Gentiles" (Isa. 42:6). In what ways did they fail to be this light? What might have been different about their story if Israel had continued to be faithful to the terms of God's covenant (Deut. 27—30)?

From the Commentary

> Solomon is remembered as the king during whose reign the temple was built (1 Kings 5—7; 2 Chron. 2—4). His alliance with Hiram, king of Tyre, gave him access to fine timber and skilled workmen. But he also built his own palace (1 Kings 7:1–12), which seems to have consisted of living quarters plus "the house of the forest of Lebanon," where arms were stored and displayed (10:16–17), the Hall of pillars, and the Hall of Judgment. He also built a house in Jerusalem for his Egyptian princess wife (2 Chron. 8:11). Official state visitors were overwhelmed by the splendor of these structures (1 Kings 10).
>
> —*Be Responsible*, page 34

9. Why does the Bible tell us so much about Solomon's great building accomplishments? What does his story reveal to us about the respect Solomon had for his Lord? What does it say about his own pride? Are there any parallels between Solomon as a builder of beautiful things and today's church? Explain.

From the Commentary

> King David appreciated and enjoyed God's created world and wrote hymns of praise about the Creator and His creation, but Solomon looked upon nature more as an object of study. God gave Solomon wisdom and breadth of understanding beyond that of the great wise men of the east, and he was able to lecture accurately about the living things in God's creation. Ecclesiastes 2:5 informs us that Solomon planted great gardens, and no doubt it was in these that he observed the way plants and trees developed…
>
> Peace and prosperity reigned while Solomon was king, but no matter how successful things appeared to citizens and visitors, all was not well in the kingdom. During the period between his ascension to the throne and his dedication of the temple, Solomon appears to have walked with the Lord and sought to please Him. But Alexander Whyte expressed it vividly when he wrote that "the secret worm … was gnawing all the time in the royal staff upon which Solomon leaned." Solomon didn't have the steadfast devotion to the Lord that characterized his father, and his many pagan wives were planting seeds in his heart that would bear bitter fruit.
>
> —*Be Responsible*, pages 44–45

10. Many of Solomon's writings mentioned in Scripture were lost. What does this tell us about the richness of the characters beyond what we see in

the pages of the Bible? Solomon's rule was peaceful, but clearly there were problems under the surface. What were some of those problems reflected in 1 Kings 4? What does this teach us about how to assess the quality and success of today's church?

Looking Inward

Take a moment to reflect on all that you've explored thus far in this study of 1 Kings 1—4; 1 Chronicles 29:22–30; and 2 Chronicles 1. Review your notes and answers and think about how each of these things matters in your life today.

> *Tips for Small Groups: To get the most out of this section, form pairs or trios and have group members take turns answering these questions. Be honest and as open as you can in this discussion, but most of all, be encouraging and supportive of others. Be sensitive to those who are going through particularly difficult times and don't press for people to speak if they're uncomfortable doing so.*

11. Have you ever felt as if you were "owed" a certain role or responsibility? How did you deal with that sense of entitlement? How did your faith factor into your examination of the circumstance?

12. Are you more like David or Solomon when it comes to leading others? Explain. What are some of the positive qualities of each that you would like to have? What are some of the negative attributes that you struggle with?

13. Describe a time when all appeared to be good in your life but things were falling apart under the surface. How was your spiritual life during that season? What does this reveal about the importance of your connection with God even during the "good" times?

Going Forward

14. Think of one or two things that you have learned that you'd like to work on in the coming week. Remember that this is all about quality, not quantity. It's better to work on one specific area of life and do it well than

to work on many and do poorly (or to be so overwhelmed that you simply don't try).

Do you want to attend to what is going on under the surface of your life? Be specific. Go back through 1 Kings 1—4; 1 Chronicles 29:22–30; and 2 Chronicles 1 and put a star next to the phrase or verse that is most encouraging to you. Consider memorizing this verse.

Real-Life Application Ideas: Solomon was a wise man, a learned man. This week, honor this positive characteristic by spending your quiet time reading some of the wisdom literature in the Bible (such as the books of Proverbs and Ecclesiastes) and works by wise Christians you respect. Use this time to soak up wisdom, not so you can go and "fix" things, but so you know better how to listen when people come to you with their concerns or problems.

Seeking Help

15. Write a prayer below (or simply pray one in silence), inviting God to work on your mind and heart in those areas you've noted in the Going Forward section. Be honest about your desires and fears.

Notes for Small Groups:

- *Look for ways to put into practice the things you wrote in the Going Forward section. Talk with other group members about your ideas and commit to being accountable to one another.*
- *During the coming week, ask the Holy Spirit to continue to reveal truth to you from what you've read and studied.*
- *Before you start the next lesson, read 1 Kings 5—6; 7:13–51; and 2 Chronicles 2—4. For more in-depth lesson preparation, read chapter 3, "Fulfilling David's Dream," in* Be Responsible.

David's Dream
(1 KINGS 5—6; 7:13–51; 2 CHRONICLES 2—4)

Before you begin …

- *Pray for the Holy Spirit to reveal truth and wisdom as you go through this lesson.*
- *Read 1 Kings 5—6; 7:13–51; and 2 Chronicles 2—4. This lesson references chapter 3 in* Be Responsible. *It will be helpful for you to have your Bible and a copy of the commentary available as you work through this lesson.*

Getting Started

From the Commentary

"Surely I will not come into the tabernacle of my house, nor go up into my bed; I will not give sleep to mine eyes, or slumber to mine eyelids, until I find out a place for the Lord, a habitation for the mighty God of Jacob" (Ps. 132:3–5). So wrote King David, for it was his passionate desire to build a temple for the glory of the Lord. "One thing have I desired of the Lord, that will I seek after; that

I may dwell in the house of the Lord all the days of my life, to behold the beauty of the Lord, and to inquire in his temple" (Ps. 27:4).

The Lord knew David's heart but made it clear that He had other plans for His beloved servant (2 Sam. 7). David was so busy fighting wars and expanding and defending the borders of the kingdom of Israel that he didn't have time to supervise such a complex and demanding enterprise. Solomon, the man of peace, was God's choice to build the temple.…

The nations around them had temples dedicated to their false gods, so it was only right that the people of Israel dedicate a magnificent temple to honor Jehovah of Hosts, the true and living God. In the second month (our April/May) of the year 966 BC, the fourth year of his reign, Solomon began the work, and 1 Kings 5—6 records several stages of the project.

—*Be Responsible*, pages 49–50

1. Why was the building of a temple so important to the Israelites? How did God prepare Solomon for the role of temple builder? (See 1 Chron. 22; 28.) What did the temple signify to the Israelites? What is an appropriate parallel for the temple in today's world?

More to Consider: As he anticipated the building of the temple, David had set aside some of the spoils of battle for the Lord (1 Chron. 22:14). This amounted to 3,750 tons of gold; 37,500 tons of silver; and an unmeasured amount of bronze, iron, wood, and stone. All this wealth he presented publicly to Solomon (1 Chron. 29:1–5). David also added his own personal treasure and then invited the leaders of the nation to contribute as well (1 Chron. 29:1–10). The final totals were 4,050 tons of gold and over 38,000 tons of silver, not to mention thousands of tons of bronze and iron as well as precious stones. It was a great beginning for a great project. What's the purpose of including this kind of detail in Scripture? What does it tell us about God's preparation of His people? About God's expectations for His people? About planning? About generosity?

2. Choose one verse or phrase from 1 Kings 5—6; 7:13–51; or 2 Chronicles 2—4 that stands out to you. This could be something you're intrigued by, something that makes you uncomfortable, something that puzzles you, something that resonates with you, or just something you want to examine further. Write that here.

Going Deeper

From the Commentary

> David gave Solomon the plans for the temple that had been given to him by the Lord (1 Chron. 28). David had also assembled some artisans and laborers to follow those plans and work in wood and stone to prepare material for the temple (1 Chron. 22:1–4). Hiram, king of Tyre, had provided workers and materials for the building of David's palace (2 Sam. 5:11), and David had enlisted their help in preparing wood for the temple (1 Chron. 22:4). Solomon took advantage of this royal friendship to enlist Hiram to provide the workers and timber needed for the temple.
>
> —*Be Responsible*, page 50

3. What do these preparations reveal about David's character? About what he valued most? What do they say about God's character? What do they teach us about the importance of building good friendships and relationships with others?

From the Commentary

Solomon requested a master artisan who could make the intricate and beautiful furnishings required for the temple (1 Kings 7:13–14; 2 Chron. 2:7), and King Hiram sent him Hiram (or Huram-Abi; 2 Chron. 2:13–14). He was the son of a mixed marriage, for his father was a Phoenician and his mother was from the tribe of Naphtali. He was gifted as a metal worker and cast the two pillars at the entrance of the temple as well as the metal furnishings within the temple. As when Moses built the tabernacle, the Lord assembled the needed workers and empowered them to do their work (Ex. 31:1–11; 35:30–35).

Solomon's letter was really a commercial contract, for in it he offered to pay for the wood by providing food annually for Hiram's household (1 Kings 5:11), and also to pay the workers one large payment for their labor (2 Chron. 2:10). Until the work was completed, King Hiram's household received annually 125,000 bushels of wheat and 115,000 gallons of pure olive oil. The workers would receive one payment of 125,000 bushels of wheat, 125,000 bushels of barley, and 115,000 gallons of wine and of olive oil, all of which would be divided among them. In his reply, Hiram accepted the terms and outlined the procedure. His men would cut the trees in Lebanon, prepare the logs, and then take them down the coast to Joppa (modern Jaffa; 2 Chron. 2:16), either on ships or bound together as rafts. At

> Joppa Solomon's men would claim the timber and transport it overland to the building site, about thirty-five miles away, as the crow flies.
>
> —*Be Responsible*, page 51

4. What does this story teach us about business relationships? How can we apply the wisdom from Solomon's building project to our own church projects today?

From Today's World

A church building project is almost always a contentious endeavor. Many a church has been split down the middle by such a project. Whether that's because of disagreements on how to fund it or the location or the very idea of building in the first place, building projects are fraught with controversy. Mention the phrase "building committee" to a member of any growing church and you're bound to get a spirited response, along with a story of both heroes and villains.

5. Why does a building project incite such passion (both positive and negative) in a church congregation? What are some of the biggest complaints about building projects? What are the benefits of building

a church together? What are the inherent dangers to a community of believers? How does Solomon's story of temple building inform the way we should (and shouldn't) approach such things?

From the Commentary

> It would take a great deal of manpower to fell the trees, trim the logs, and transport them to the construction site for the builders to use. David's incomplete census had revealed that there were 1,300,000 able-bodied men in the land (2 Sam. 24:9), and Solomon conscripted only 30,000 to labor on the temple, about 2.3 percent of the total available labor force. Ten thousand of the men spent one month each quarter in Lebanon assisting Hiram's men in their work, and then they had two months at home. These men were Jewish citizens and were not treated like slaves (1 Kings 9:22; see Lev. 25:39–43). We aren't told if they shared in any of the wages Solomon promised Hiram's workers, but they probably didn't.
>
> Solomon also took a census of the non-Israelite aliens in the land and drafted 150,000 of them to cut and transport stones for the temple (1 Kings 5:15–18; 9:15–23; 2 Chron.

> 2:17–18; 8:7–10). Of this group, 70,000 carried burdens and 80,000 cut limestone blocks from the hills. In charge of this group were 3,000 overseers and 300 supervisors who were aliens, and over the entire group were 250 Jewish officers. The stone blocks had to be cut carefully so they would fit together perfectly when assembled at the temple site (1 Kings 6:7), and that would demand careful planning and expert supervision.
>
> —*Be Responsible*, page 52

6. What does the way Solomon treated the workers tell us about his leadership? Why is it significant that he enlisted non-Israelites to help with the project? In what ways did Solomon's decision to conscript so many workers affect the people's view of him as leader?

From the Commentary

> Hiram's workmen in Lebanon were not worshippers of the Lord, and the aliens in the land of Israel were not Jewish proselytes, yet God used both of these groups of "outsiders" to help build His holy temple. The Lord

would "have all men to be saved" (1 Tim. 2:4), but even if they aren't believers, He can use them to fulfill His purposes. He used Nebuchadnezzar and the Babylonian army to chasten Israel, and called Nebuchadnezzar "my servant" (Jer. 25:9), and He used Cyrus king of Persia to set Israel free and help them rebuild their temple (Ezra 1). This should encourage us in our praying and serving, for the Lord can use people we least appreciate to get His will done on earth.

—*Be Responsible*, page 53

7. Why does God so often use nonbelievers to accomplish His purposes? What does this reveal about God's heart? About what He expects of us in relation to those nonbelievers?

From the Commentary

What were David's two greatest sins? Most people would reply, "His adultery with Bathsheba and his taking a census of the people," and their answers would be correct. As a result of his sin of numbering the people, David

> purchased property on Mount Moriah where he built an altar and worshipped the Lord (2 Sam. 24). David married Bathsheba, and God gave them a son whom they named Solomon (2 Sam. 12:24–25). Now we have Solomon building a temple on David's property on Mount Moriah!
>
> —*Be Responsible*, page 54

8. How does God take the consequences of David's two sins and turn them into something good? Read Romans 5:20. How does this verse apply to the building of the temple? What does this teach us about God's grace?

More to Consider: The ancient world had a "short cubit" or "common cubit" of almost eighteen inches and a "long cubit" of almost twenty-one inches. The common cubit was used for the temple (2 Chron. 3:3), which meant that the structure was ninety feet long, thirty feet wide, and forty-five feet high. A porch thirty feet wide and fifteen feet deep stood at the front of the temple, and a courtyard for the priests surrounded the sanctuary. It was separated from an outer courtyard by a wall composed of stone blocks and wood (1 Kings 6:36; 2 Chron. 4:9). Jeremiah 36:10 calls the court of the priests "the upper courtyard," which suggests that it stood higher than the outer courtyard. The doors of the temple faced east, as did the gate of the tabernacle. What does this detailed description of the temple teach us about God's relationship with His people in the day of David and Solomon? Why would God give such detailed plans to His people? Does God still communicate with His people the same way today? Explain.

From the Commentary

> We don't know who brought the message in 1 Kings 6:11–13 (probably a prophet) or when it was delivered, but the Lord sent His Word to the king at a time when he was either discouraged with the building program or (more likely) starting to become proud of what he was accomplishing. The Lord reminded Solomon, as He must constantly remind us, that He's not impressed with our work if our walk isn't obedient to Him. What He wants is an obedient heart (Eph. 6:6). God would fulfill His promises to David and Solomon (2 Sam. 7), not because Solomon built the temple but because he obeyed the Word of the Lord. A similar warning was included in the covenant God gave Moses in Deuteronomy 28—30, so it was not a new revelation to Solomon. This was the second time God spoke to Solomon about obedience (1 Kings 3:5ff.), and He would speak to him about it again after the dedication of the temple (9:3–9).
>
> —*Be Responsible*, page 55

9. Review 1 Kings 6:11–13. Which would have been a more dangerous place to be—discouraged about the building or prideful about the building? How does God deal with discouragement? Pride? How does God repeatedly teach His people about the importance of obedience?

From the Commentary

> It's difficult to calculate the cost of this building in modern currency. It isn't enough just to know the price of the precious metal today, but we also need to know its purchasing power. Then we must calculate what Solomon paid for manpower and materials and try to express it in contemporary equivalents. When you consider that there was gold overlay on the inside walls and floors, the furniture, the doors, and the cherubim, you have no hesitation concluding that this was a very costly building. And yet all this beauty was destroyed and this wealth was confiscated when the Babylonian army captured Jerusalem and destroyed the temple (see Jer. 52). Nebuchadnezzar robbed the temple and deported the captives in stages, and eventually his men burned the city and the temple so they could get their hands on all the gold that was there.

How painful it is to realize that Solomon, the man who constructed the temple, was the man who married a multitude of foreign wives and encouraged idolatry in Israel, the very sin that turned the nation away from God and brought upon them the fiery judgment of the Lord.

—*Be Responsible*, page 60

10. In what ways was Solomon responsible for the eventual destruction of the temple? How could someone so wise have been such a fool when it came to knowing how to honor God and lead His people? What are the character flaws that led to Solomon's errors of judgment?

Looking Inward

Take a moment to reflect on all that you've explored thus far in this study of 1 Kings 5—6; 7:13–51; and 2 Chronicles 2—4. Review your notes and answers and think about how each of these things matters in your life today.

Tips for Small Groups: To get the most out of this section, form pairs or trios and have group members take turns answering these questions. Be honest and as open as you can in this discussion, but most of all, be encouraging and supportive of others. Be sensitive to those who are going through particularly difficult times and don't press for people to speak if they're uncomfortable doing so.

11. What are some ways God has used nonbelievers to grow your faith? How has that changed the way you look at those who do not believe as you do?

12. Have you ever been a part of a church building project? Describe that experience. What good came from it? What were the challenges and obstacles? How did your faith grow because of that experience?

13. What are some ways pride has intruded on your relationship with God? What are some of the things you're prideful about? What is the eventual result of your prideful choices?

Going Forward

14. Think of one or two things that you have learned that you'd like to work on in the coming week. Remember that this is all about quality, not quantity. It's better to work on one specific area of life and do it well than to work on many and do poorly (or to be so overwhelmed that you simply don't try).

Do you want to take some steps toward being a strong but humbler leader? Be specific. Go back through 1 Kings 5—6; 7:13–51; and 2 Chronicles 2—4 and put a star next to the phrase or verse that is most encouraging to you. Consider memorizing this verse.

Real-Life Application Ideas: This week, take on a building project of your own. Invite the whole family or a group of friends to participate with you. You might build an actual building (that storage shed you've always wanted) or a garden or perhaps something a bit more symbolic (such as a model). Or you could choose to donate your time and skills to help someone else with a building project. As you work on this project, focus your attention not on getting things done but on thankfulness for God's provision. Spend plenty of time in prayer throughout the experience, listening for God's direction even in the little things.

Seeking Help

15. Write a prayer below (or simply pray one in silence), inviting God to work on your mind and heart in those areas you've noted in the Going Forward section. Be honest about your desires and fears.

Notes for Small Groups:

- *Look for ways to put into practice the things you wrote in the Going Forward section. Talk with other group members about your ideas and commit to being accountable to one another.*
- *During the coming week, ask the Holy Spirit to continue to reveal truth to you from what you've read and studied.*
- *Before you start the next lesson, read 1 Kings 8:1—9:9, 25–28; and 2 Chronicles 5—7. For more in-depth lesson preparation, read chapter 4, "God's House and Solomon's Heart," in* Be Responsible.

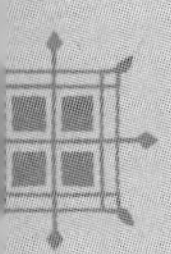

Solomon's Heart
(1 KINGS 8:1—9:9, 25–28; 2 CHRONICLES 5—7)

Before you begin …

- *Pray for the Holy Spirit to reveal truth and wisdom as you go through this lesson.*
- *Read 1 Kings 8:1—9:9, 25–28; and 2 Chronicles 5—7. This lesson references chapter 4 in* Be Responsible. *It will be helpful for you to have your Bible and a copy of the commentary available as you work through this lesson.*

Getting Started

From the Commentary

"Fellow citizens, we cannot escape history." Abraham Lincoln spoke those words to the American Congress on December 1, 1862, but King Solomon could have spoken them to the Jewish leaders when he dedicated the temple during the Feast of Tabernacles in the twenty-fourth year of his reign.

> No matter where the Jews are in this world, or what the century is, they have their roots in Abraham, Moses, and David. King David is mentioned twelve times in 1 Kings 8:1—9:9, and Moses is mentioned three times. During his prayer, Solomon referred to God's covenant with his father (2 Sam. 7) and also to the covenant God gave to Moses recorded in Deuteronomy 28—30.
>
> —*Be Responsible*, page 63

1. What is the main thrust of Solomon's prayer? Read Deuteronomy 30:1–10. How does the promise in this passage inform Solomon's prayer?

More to Consider: Israel's kings were commanded to make their own copies of the book of Deuteronomy (Deut. 17:18–20). What do Solomon's many references to Deuteronomy indicate about how well he knew that book? Why would that particular book be so important to Solomon? How did it direct his ways? What are some ways he might have missed its message?

2. Choose one verse or phrase from 1 Kings 8:1—9:9, 25–28; or 2 Chronicles 5—7 that stands out to you. This could be something you're intrigued by, something that makes you uncomfortable, something that puzzles you, something that resonates with you, or just something you want to examine further. Write that here.

Going Deeper

From the Commentary

> Solomon assembled at Jerusalem the leaders of the tribes of Israel and whoever of the citizens could attend, from the north to south (1 Kings 8:65), that they might assist him in dedicating the house of God. The word "house" is used twenty-six times in 1 Kings 8:1—9:9 (thirty-seven times in 2 Chron. 5—7), for this structure was indeed the "house of God" (1 Kings 8:10, 11, 17, etc.). But what made this costly building the house of the Lord? Not simply that God commanded it to be built and chose Solomon to build it, or that He gave the plans to David and provided the wealth to construct it.
>
> —*Be Responsible*, page 64

3. Note the uses of the word "house" or "temple" in 1 Kings 8:1–11. What is the significance of using this word? What made the temple the house of the Lord? Why was it important to God's people for their Lord to have a "house" they could see and touch?

From the Commentary

In the Holy of Holies, Jehovah was "enthroned between the cherubim" (Ps. 80:1 NIV). The pagan nations had their temples, altars, priests, and sacrifices, but their temples were empty and their sacrifices useless. The true and living God dwelt in the temple on Mount Moriah! That's why Solomon's first act of dedication was to have the ark of the covenant brought from the tent David had pitched for it (2 Sam. 6:17) and placed into the inner sanctuary of the temple. The tabernacle equipment and furnishings were also brought to the temple and stored there (2 Chron. 5:5). The ark of the covenant was the only piece of the original furniture that was kept in active service, for nothing could replace the throne of God or the law of God that was kept in the ark. That this dedication service took place during the Feast of Tabernacles was significant, for the ark had led Israel all during their wilderness journey.

The priests placed the ark before the large cherubim that Hiram had made, whose wings spanned the width of the Holy of Holies (1 Kings 6:23–30). The cherubim on the original golden mercy seat looked at each other, while the new cherubim looked out toward the Holy Place where the priests ministered. The angels of God not only "look into" the mysteries of God's grace (1 Peter 1:12), but they also behold the ministry of God's people and learn about God's grace (1 Cor. 4:9; 11:10; Eph. 3:10; 1 Tim. 5:21). At one time, a pot of manna and the staff of Aaron stood before the ark (Ex. 16:33; Num. 17:10; Heb. 9:4), both of which were reminders of rebellion in Israel (Ex. 16:1–3; Num. 16). But the nation was now making a new beginning and those items weren't needed. The important thing was that Israel obey the law of God that was kept in the ark.

—*Be Responsible*, pages 64–65

4. Why was the ark the only element from the traveling days that the Israelites kept in active service? Why was it such an important reminder for them? Why were the staves, or "carrying poles," left attached to the ark, even after the Israelites were no longer a pilgrim people carrying the ark with them as they traveled?

From Today's World

Aside from its starring role in a blockbuster movie, the ark of the covenant is little more than a footnote for today's Christians. It represents a time when God's people looked to a singular place—first the tabernacle, then the temple—to find God. Today's church building is nothing like the temple; it's a place for all believers, not just the priests. But many churches do hold some furnishings with great regard, such as an altar or a cross or some other significant piece usually placed at the front of the sanctuary for all to see.

5. What are some of the ways today's church honors the history and significance of the ancient temple? Do churchgoers today expect to meet God more fully inside a building than outside? Explain. What are the benefits of having a church building rather than simply meeting as the church in homes or elsewhere? What are the potential risks of making the church building itself a holy place?

From the Commentary

> The ark was but a symbol of the throne and presence of God; it was the actual presence of the Lord in His house that was important. Once Solomon and the people had

> honored God and placed His throne in the Holy of Holies, the glory of God came and filled the house of the Lord. The glory cloud had guided Israel through the wilderness (Num. 9:15–23), but now the glory came to dwell within the beautiful temple Solomon had built. As the glory filled the house, the priests praised God with voices and instruments, for the Lord inhabits the praises of His people (Ps. 22:3).
>
> —*Be Responsible*, page 65

6. In what ways was the presence of God's glory the distinguishing mark of Israel? (See Ex. 33:12–23; Rom. 9:4.) How did the sins of the people cause God's glory to depart from the tabernacle? (See 1 Sam. 4:19–22.) What must it have been like for the Israelites finally to have God's glory returned to them with the construction of the temple?

From the Commentary

> God not only graciously dwells with His people, but He also gives them His Word and faithfully keeps His promises. That's the major theme of 1 Kings 8:12–21 and

> 2 Chronicles 6:1–11, for in it Solomon glorified Jehovah by reviewing the history of the building of the temple.…
>
> Like a servant reporting to his master, Solomon announced that he had built the house to be God's dwelling place (1 Kings 8:13). This reminds us that Moses finished the work of building and erecting the tabernacle (Ex. 40:33), that our Savior finished all that the Father instructed Him to do (John 17:4), and that both John the Baptist and Paul finished their courses successfully (Acts 13:25; 2 Tim. 4:7). All of us will give an account of our life and service when we see the Lord (Rom. 14:10–13), and it behooves us to be faithful to the calling He has given us, so that we end well.
>
> —*Be Responsible*, pages 66–67

7. Review 1 Kings 8:12–21. How did Solomon glorify the Lord? What did reviewing the building of the temple reveal about the Israelites? About faithfulness? Why was it important for Solomon to go over this history with God's people? What did it teach them about God?

From the Commentary

> God in His goodness and grace made a covenant with David concerning his family and his throne (2 Sam. 7), and He included in that covenant the promise of a son who would build the temple. What God spoke with His mouth, He accomplished with His hand (1 Kings 8:15), and what He promised to David, He performed through Solomon (v. 20). But God did these things for the honor of His name, not for the glory of either David or Solomon (vv. 16–20).
>
> —*Be Responsible*, page 68

8. God's name is referred to several times in Solomon's address and prayer. What does this tell us about Solomon's understanding of God's role in building the temple? In what ways was the temple to be a reminder of God's faithfulness and goodness? Is today's church a similar reminder? Explain.

More to Consider: According to 2 Chronicles 6:13, Solomon knelt on the special platform near the altar as he prayed this prayer, his hands lifted to heaven. Our traditional posture for prayer (hands folded and eyes closed) was unknown to the Jews. Their posture was to look up by faith toward God in heaven (or toward the temple) and lift their open hands to show their poverty and their expectancy as they awaited the answer (1 Kings 8:38, 54; Ex. 9:29, 33; Ps. 63:4; 88:9; 143:6). Why might this practice have been carried over into the early church (1 Tim. 2:8)? What is the significance of the word "heaven" used more than a dozen times in 1 Kings 8:22–54?

From the Commentary

> As Solomon prayed, he was overwhelmed by the contrast between the greatness of God and the insignificance of the work he had done in building the temple. How could Almighty God, the God of the heavens, dwell in a building made by men's hands? Solomon had expressed this same truth to King Hiram before he began to build (2 Chron. 2:6), and the prophet Isaiah echoed it (Isa. 66:1). Stephen referred to these words from Solomon and Isaiah when he defended himself before the Jewish council (Acts 7:47–50), and Paul emphasized this truth when preaching to the Gentiles (Acts 17:24).
>
> —*Be Responsible*, page 69

9. Review 1 Kings 8:22–53. In what ways was Solomon's prayer recognition of God's grace? What requests did Solomon bring to the Lord in this prayer? What was his final request of God? How is this an appropriate prayer for us today?

From the Commentary

> The king had been kneeling on the special platform near the altar, his hands lifted to God, but now he stood to give the people a blessing from the Lord. Usually it was the priests who blessed the people (Num. 6:22–27), but on a special occasion such as this, the king could give the blessing as David did (2 Sam. 6:18, 20). Solomon blessed the whole assembly and through them the entire nation, and he gave thanks to God for His great mercies.
>
> As Solomon reviewed the history of the Jewish nation, his conclusion was that the promises of God had never failed, not even once.
>
> —*Be Responsible*, pages 74–75

10. What were some of the promises that God had made to His people? What does this conclusion from Solomon reveal about the history of the Israelites? Why did Solomon emphasize the promise that God would never leave nor forsake them? Why is this an important promise for us in today's church?

Looking Inward

Take a moment to reflect on all that you've explored thus far in this study of 1 Kings 8:1—9:9, 25–28; and 2 Chronicles 5—7. Review your notes and answers and think about how each of these things matters in your life today.

> *Tips for Small Groups: To get the most out of this section, form pairs or trios and have group members take turns answering these questions. Be honest and as open as you can in this discussion, but most of all, be encouraging and supportive of others. Be sensitive to those who are going through particularly difficult times and don't press for people to speak if they're uncomfortable doing so.*

11. What impresses you most about Solomon's accomplishments? What parts of his prayer do you relate to most? How is Solomon's relationship with God similar to yours? How is it different?

12. Do you feel God's presence more in some places than others? Explain. How does God use these places to make Himself more known to you? What does this teach you about God's nearness? What does it teach you about yourself?

13. How have God's promises influenced your daily life? What are some of His promises you are most thankful for? How can trusting God's promises help you through difficult times?

Going Forward

14. Think of one or two things that you have learned that you'd like to work on in the coming week. Remember that this is all about quality, not quantity. It's better to work on one specific area of life and do it well than to work on many and do poorly (or to be so overwhelmed that you simply don't try).

Do you want to spend more time in God's presence worshipping Him? Be specific. Go back through 1 Kings 8:1—9:9, 25–28; and 2 Chronicles 5—7 and put a star next to the phrase or verse that is most encouraging to you. Consider memorizing this verse.

Real-Life Application Ideas: What does it mean to you to glorify God? How does that look in everyday life? Use this week to glorify God in all the ways you can come up with. Start by being thankful for all He has provided for you—a place to live, food to eat, friends, community. Then consider what it means to glorify God wherever you happen to be—at home, at work, among strangers, in a crowded coffee shop. Be conscious of God's presence in all of those places this week.

Seeking Help

15. Write a prayer below (or simply pray one in silence), inviting God to work on your mind and heart in those areas you've noted in the Going Forward section. Be honest about your desires and fears.

Notes for Small Groups:

- *Look for ways to put into practice the things you wrote in the Going Forward section. Talk with other group members about your ideas and commit to being accountable to one another.*
- *During the coming week, ask the Holy Spirit to continue to reveal truth to you from what you've read and studied.*
- *Before you start the next lesson, read 1 Kings 7:1–12; 9:10—10:29; 11; and 2 Chronicles 8—9. For more in-depth lesson preparation, read chapters 5 and 6, "The Kingdom, Power, and Glory" and "The Foolish Wise Man," in* Be Responsible.

Power and Glory

(1 KINGS 7:1–12; 9:10—10:29; 11; 2 CHRONICLES 8—9)

Before you begin …

- *Pray for the Holy Spirit to reveal truth and wisdom as you go through this lesson.*
- *Read 1 Kings 7:1–12; 9:10—10:29; 11; and 2 Chronicles 8—9. This lesson references chapters 5 and 6 in* Be Responsible. *It will be helpful for you to have your Bible and a copy of the commentary available as you work through this lesson.*

Getting Started

From the Commentary

> Most people remember King Solomon as the man who built the temple of God in Jerusalem, but during his reign, he was occupied with many different activities. These chapters record a series of vignettes depicting some of the things Solomon did to advance his kingdom and enhance his life. But these activities also reveal Solomon's

> character and expose some of the areas of weakness that later produced a bitter harvest. Gradually, Solomon became more interested in prices than in values, and in reputation rather than character, and in the splendor of the kingdom rather than the good of the people and the glory of the Lord.
>
> —*Be Responsible*, page 83

1. What contributed to the shift in Solomon's character? How is this similar to the way leaders today (not just in churches) find themselves tempted to focus more on reputation and splendor, or appearance of wealth, rather than good character?

More to Consider: The work on the temple structure was completed in seven years, but it took several more years for Hiram and his crew to decorate the interior and construct the furnishings. While they were busy at the temple, Solomon designed and built a palace for himself that was a combination of personal residence, city hall, armory, and official reception center. "I undertook great projects," he wrote, "I built houses for myself" (Eccl. 2:4). Why did Solomon need a resplendent palace for himself? What does this reveal about his heart? His priorities? How is this similar or dissimilar to the way leaders of big churches approach the quality of their own lives? Is this a concern? Why or why not?

2. Choose one verse or phrase from 1 Kings 7:1–12; 9:10—10:29; 11; or 2 Chronicles 8—9 that stands out to you. This could be something you're intrigued by, something that makes you uncomfortable, something that puzzles you, something that resonates with you, or just something you want to examine further. Write that here.

Going Deeper

From the Commentary

Hiram, king of Tyre, had been David's good friend, and David had told him about his plans to build a temple for the Lord (1 Kings 5:1–3), plans the Lord didn't permit David to carry out. After David's death, Solomon became Hiram's friend (Prov. 27:10) and contracted with Hiram to help build the temple (1 Kings 5:1–12). Hiram would send timber and workers if Solomon would pay the workers and provide Hiram with food in return for the timber. Solomon also conscripted Jewish men to cut stone (5:13–18) and the aliens in the land to help bear burdens (9:15, 20–23; 2 Chron. 8:7–10).

But 1 Kings 9:11 and 14 inform us that Hiram also supplied Solomon with 120 talents of gold (about four and a half tons)! King Solomon had at least 3,750 tons of gold available before he began to build the temple (1 Chron. 22:14–16), and the fact that he had to get gold from Hiram surprises us. The gold, silver, and other materials for the temple that are inventoried in 1 Chronicles 22; 28—29 were all dedicated to the Lord, so they couldn't be used for any other building. This means Solomon needed the gold for the "palace" complex, perhaps for the gold shields, so he borrowed it from Hiram, giving him the twenty cities as collateral. These cities were conveniently located on the border of Phoenicia and Galilee.

—*Be Responsible*, pages 85–86

3. Review 1 Kings 9:10–14. Why was Solomon wrong to give twenty cities away to pay his debts? (See Lev. 25:23.) What does this say about the extravagance of his building projects? In what ways is this situation similar to modern scandals in which people in power use money that's not really theirs to enhance their own lives?

From the Commentary

> When the Lord appeared to Solomon in Gibeon, He promised to give him riches and honor to such an extent that there would be no king like him all the days of his life (1 Kings 3:13). He kept that promise and made Solomon's name famous and his accomplishments admired by people in other nations. Solomon's father, David, had conquered enemy territory and added it to the kingdom, but he hadn't attempted to build an international network that would make Israel powerful among the nations. David was a mighty general who feared no enemy, but Solomon was a shrewd diplomat and politician who missed no opportunity to increase his wealth and power.
>
> —*Be Responsible*, pages 86–87

4. Review 1 Kings 9:15–28. What are some of the achievements listed in this section? What do these accomplishments tell us about Solomon's power and influence? About his goals as king?

From the Commentary

The record of the Queen of Sheba's visit (1 Kings 10:1–13) gives us an opportunity to get a glimpse of life in the palace. The queen not only marveled at Solomon's palace, but she was impressed by the meals (1 Kings 4:7, 22–23), the livery and conduct of the servants, the seating of the officers and guests, and the incredible wealth that was displayed on and around the tables. She walked with Solomon on his private concourse to the temple where she watched him worship. (See 10:5 and 2 Chron. 9:4 NIV margin.) The wisdom of Solomon's words and the wealth of Solomon's kingdom were just too much for her, and she was no pauper herself! She brought Solomon expensive gifts, including an abundance of spices and 120 talents of gold (four and a half tons). Solomon reciprocated by giving her whatever she asked for out of his royal bounty.

The queen couldn't contain herself. She announced publicly that Solomon and his servants had to be the happiest

> people on earth, yet it was Solomon who later wrote the book of Ecclesiastes and declared, "Vanity of vanities, all is vanity!" We wonder if Solomon's officers and servants didn't gradually grow accustomed to all the pomp and circumstance of court life, especially the gaudy display of wealth. Even Solomon wrote, "Better is a little with the fear of the Lord, than great treasure with trouble. Better is a dinner of herbs [vegetables] where love is, than a fatted calf with hatred" (Prov. 15:16–17 NKJV).
>
> —*Be Responsible*, page 90

5. Why was the Queen of Sheba so impressed by Solomon's temple? What does this story reveal about what was going on behind the scenes in Solomon's heart? Read Matthew 12:39–42. Why did Jesus commend the queen, even though she went back home to worship her own gods?

From the Commentary

> When God promised to give Solomon wisdom, He also promised him riches and honor (1 Kings 3:13). It isn't a sin to possess wealth or to inherit wealth. Abraham was a very wealthy man who gave all his wealth to his son

Isaac (Gen. 24:34–36). Earning money honestly isn't a sin, but loving money and living just to acquire riches is a sin (1 Tim. 6:7–10).

Solomon himself wrote, "Whoever loves money never has money enough; whoever loves wealth is never satisfied with his income. This too is meaningless" (Eccl. 5:10 NIV). Someone has wisely said, "It's good to have the things that money can buy, provided you don't lose the things money can't buy."

Solomon's annual income was 666 talents of gold, or about twenty-five tons. It came from several sources: (1) taxes, (2) tolls, customs, and duty fees, (3) trade, (4) tribute from vassal rulers, and (5) gifts. His use of conscripted labor was also a form of income. It took a great deal of money to support his splendid manner of life, and after Solomon's death, the people of Israel protested the yoke they were wearing and asked for the burden to be lightened (1 Kings 12:1–15).

—*Be Responsible*, page 92

6. Why did Solomon need an ivory throne overlaid with gold? Why did he and his guests have to drink only from golden vessels? Why did he need seven hundred wives and three hundred concubines? How was Solomon's pursuit of wealth and opulence a direct disobedience of God's will for His people? What went wrong for Solomon to go from obedience to selfishness? How is this similar to the path people often take in today's world?

From the Commentary

> The danger of marrying pagan unbelievers is spelled out in 1 Kings 11:2 NKJV, which is an allusion to Deuteronomy 7:4: "they will turn away your hearts after their gods." That's exactly what happened to Solomon (1 Kings 11:3, 4, 9). The Ammonites and Moabites were descendants of Abraham's nephew Lot (Gen. 19:30ff.). The Ammonites worshipped the hideous god Molech and sacrificed their infants on his altars (Lev. 18:21; 20:1–5; and see Jer. 7:29–34; Ezek. 16:20–22). Chemosh was the chief god of the Moabites, and Ashtereth (Astarte) was the goddess of the people of Tyre and Sidon. As the goddess of fertility, her worship included "legalized prostitution" involving both male and female temple prostitutes, and that worship was unspeakably filthy. (See Deut. 23:1–8; 1 Kings 14:24; 15:12; 22:46.) The Babylonians also worshipped this goddess and called her Ishtar.
>
> Solomon had exhorted the people to have hearts that were "perfect with the Lord" (8:61), that is, undivided and totally yielded to Him alone; yet his own heart wasn't perfect with God (11:4).
>
> —*Be Responsible*, pages 98–99

7. Solomon didn't totally abandon Jehovah but made Him one of the many gods he worshipped (1 Kings 9:25). How was this a direct violation of the first two commandments given at Sinai? (See Ex. 20:1–6; Isa. 46:9.) In what ways was Solomon's compromise a slow slide rather than a sudden change? (See Ps. 1:1.) How is this similar to the way people often slide into worldliness today?

From the Commentary

> The Lord wasn't impressed with Solomon's royal splendor, for the Lord looks on the heart (1 Sam. 16:7) and searches the heart (1 Chron. 28:9; Jer. 17:10; Rev. 2:23). It was Solomon who wrote, "Keep your heart with all diligence, for out of it spring the issues of life" (Prov. 4:23 NKJV), yet in his old age, his own heart was far from the Lord. Since the discovery of the circulation of the blood by William Harvey in the 17th century, everybody knows that the center of human physical life is the heart. But what's true physically is also true morally and spiritually. We're to love God with all our heart (Deut. 6:5) and receive His Word into our hearts (Prov. 7:1–3).
>
> —*Be Responsible*, page 100

8. How did Solomon's heart stray from God? Read Ephesians 6:6. What does this verse teach us about the heart? Do riches and wealth matter to God? Why or why not?

More to Consider: Twice the Lord appeared to Solomon (1 Kings 3:5; 9:2) and reminded him of the terms of the covenant He had made with Solomon's father (2 Sam. 7). Solomon certainly knew the terms of the covenant in Deuteronomy 28—30, for he referred to them in his prayer when he dedicated the temple. So what happened? Why did he lose sight of those terms? How does this serve as a warning for us today?

From the Commentary

> Solomon's many marriages had been his guarantees of peace with the neighboring rulers, and Solomon's reign had been a peaceful one. But now his system would start to fall apart, for the Lord raised up "adversaries" against Solomon (1 Kings 11:14, 23, 25) and used them to discipline the rebellious king. That God would discipline David's disobedient heirs was a part of the covenant (2 Sam. 7:14–15) and was reaffirmed to Solomon when God spoke to him at Gibeon (1 Kings 3:14). It was repeated while Solomon was building the temple (6:11–13) and after the temple was dedicated (9:3–9). See also 1 Chronicles 22:10 and Psalm 89:30–37. The king certainly could not have been ignorant of the dangers of disobeying the Lord.
>
> —*Be Responsible*, page 102

9. Review 1 Kings 11:14–25. Who are some of the adversaries listed in this section? In what ways did God "raise them up" to help discipline the Israelites? Why did God often allow or even direct enemies to attack His people? Does God operate the same way today? Explain.

From the Commentary

> Like King Saul, Solomon was handed great opportunities but didn't make the most of them. He knew a great deal about animals, plants, bringing wealth to the nation, and constructing buildings, but he was defective in sharing the knowledge of the Lord with the Gentiles who came to his throne room. Like his father, David, Solomon had a gift for enjoying women, but when Solomon sinned, he didn't have David's sincere heart and broken spirit of repentance. The grandeur of the kingdom and not the glory of the Lord was what motivated Solomon's life.
>
> He left behind the temple of God, his royal palace, a nation in bondage, an economy in trouble, as well as the books of Proverbs, Ecclesiastes, and the Song of Solomon. The nation was united during his reign, but there was a hairline split in the nation that eventually revealed itself in open rebellion and division.
>
> —*Be Responsible*, pages 105–6

10. In what ways did Solomon's hunger for wealth and achievement lead to a revolt by the people? What were other ways the people reacted to Solomon's disobedience? How did they mimic his behavior toward the foreign nations? What does this teach us about the influence of a leader, especially when that leader is making poor decisions?

Looking Inward

Take a moment to reflect on all that you've explored thus far in this study of 1 Kings 7:1–12; 9:10—10:29; 11; and 2 Chronicles 8—9. Review your notes and answers and think about how each of these things matters in your life today.

Tips for Small Groups: To get the most out of this section, form pairs or trios and have group members take turns answering these questions. Be honest and as open as you can in this discussion, but most of all, be encouraging and supportive of others. Be sensitive to those who are going through particularly difficult times and don't press for people to speak if they're uncomfortable doing so.

11. How have your circumstances affected your character? Have you responded well to times of lacking? Times of plenty? Why is it important to have a strong, humble faith regardless of your situation?

12. Describe a time when you were truly proud of your achievements. What's the difference between a healthy pride and a pride that comes before a fall? How do you keep your pride in check?

13. What are some of the ways you're tempted by the pursuit of wealth? Why do material things seem important to you? If you are struggling financially, how can that lead you to a closer relationship with God? If you're in a season of plenty, how can that lead you closer to God?

Going Forward

14. Think of one or two things that you have learned that you'd like to work on in the coming week. Remember that this is all about quality, not quantity. It's better to work on one specific area of life and do it well than to work on many and do poorly (or to be so overwhelmed that you simply don't try).

Do you want to make a good decision about wealth? Be specific. Go back through 1 Kings 7:1–12; 9:10—10:29; 11; and 2 Chronicles 8—9 and put a star next to the phrase or verse that is most encouraging to you. Consider memorizing this verse.

Real-Life Application Ideas: Much of this section in 1 Kings is focused on Solomon's slow fade from favor to a life of disobedience. And much of that slide seemed to come from his relentless pursuit of material wealth. This week, take a hard look at your pursuit of material things. Sift through your needs and wants and ask God to help you determine a proper approach to your finances and material goods. Be intentional with every penny you spend, asking for God's wisdom to help you make wise choices. Then at the end of the week, take stock of the lessons you learned and apply them as you move forward in life.

Seeking Help

15. Write a prayer below (or simply pray one in silence), inviting God to work on your mind and heart in those areas you've noted in the Going Forward section. Be honest about your desires and fears.

Notes for Small Groups:

- *Look for ways to put into practice the things you wrote in the Going Forward section. Talk with other group members about your ideas and commit to being accountable to one another.*
- *During the coming week, ask the Holy Spirit to continue to reveal truth to you from what you've read and studied.*
- *Before you start the next lesson, read 1 Kings 12:1–24; 14:21–31; and 2 Chronicles 10—12. For more in-depth lesson preparation, read chapter 7, "He Would Not Listen," in* Be Responsible.

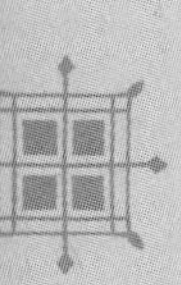

Listen

(1 KINGS 12:1–24; 14:21–31; 2 CHRONICLES 10—12)

Before you begin …

- *Pray for the Holy Spirit to reveal truth and wisdom as you go through this lesson.*
- *Read 1 Kings 12:1–24; 14:21–31; and 2 Chronicles 10—12. This lesson references chapter 7 in* Be Responsible. *It will be helpful for you to have your Bible and a copy of the commentary available as you work through this lesson.*

Getting Started

From the Commentary

"Then I hated all my labor in which I toiled under the sun," Solomon wrote in Ecclesiastes, "because I must leave it to the man who will come after me. And who knows whether he will be wise or a fool?" (Eccl. 2:18–19 NKJV).

His successor was his son Rehoboam, who occasionally made a shrewd decision but for the most part was

> a foolish ruler. At the beginning of Rehoboam's reign, a selfish decision on his part divided the nation, and during his fourth year, Rehoboam decided to turn from the Lord and worship idols, and that brought the judgment of the Lord. His reign could hardly be called successful.
>
> —*Be Responsible*, page 109

1. What was the selfish decision Rehoboam made early in his reign? Why did it divide the nation? What are some of the reasons his reign was a failure?

2. Choose one verse or phrase from 1 Kings 12:1–24; 14:21–31; or 2 Chronicles 10—12 that stands out to you. This could be something you're intrigued by, something that makes you uncomfortable, something that puzzles you, something that resonates with you, or just something you want to examine further. Write that here.

Going Deeper

From the Commentary

> Alexander Maclaren called the account in 1 Kings 12:1–17 (and 2 Chron. 10:1–19) "a miserable story of imbecility and arrogance," and he was right. The story reveals that, whatever gifts Rehoboam may have possessed, he didn't have the gift of relating to people and understanding their needs. David was a king who loved his people and risked his life for their welfare. Solomon was a king who didn't serve the people but used the people to satisfy his own desires. Rehoboam was a king who ignored the lessons of the past and turned his ears away from the voices of the suffering people.
>
> —*Be Responsible*, page 110

3. Why was Rehoboam unfit to rule? Can leaders be successful if they can't relate to the people? Why or why not? What does this tell us about the importance of a person's character in his or her ability to lead?

More to Consider: Solomon must have made it clear that Rehoboam was to be the next king, but it was still necessary for the people to affirm the choice and enter into covenant with God and the king. This had been done when Saul became king (1 Sam. 10:17–27) and also when David and Solomon were each crowned (2 Sam. 2:4; 5:1–5; 1 Kings 1:28–53). What was the purpose of having the people affirm the choice? In what ways were they entering a covenant with both God and the king? Why would God allow a clearly unfit man to be the leader of His people?

From the Commentary

> Led by Jeroboam, the leaders of the northern tribes protested the heavy yoke that Rehoboam's father had laid on them, including high taxes and forced labor. When Solomon reorganized the land into twelve districts (1 Kings 4:7–19), it appears that Judah wasn't included, and this policy may have been followed when he conscripted laborers (5:13–18). We can easily understand how the other tribes would respond to such blatant favoritism. Why should these hardworking people sacrifice just so the king could live in a magnificent house, be pampered by servants, and eat daily at a festive table? The people were wearing a galling yoke, and they were tired of it.
>
> —*Be Responsible*, pages 111–12

4. How did the people of the north respond to the choice of Rehoboam as king? What concerned them most about this decision? What are some

examples today of the challenges facing a leader whose father or mother left a questionable legacy?

From Today's World

Many churches today began as family affairs. There are certainly plenty of good reasons for family members to get involved in a church run by the patriarch or matriarch of a family. Though it could be argued that churches are breeding grounds for nepotism, it's probably true that family members' involvement comes out of a shared commitment to preaching the gospel and spreading the good news. Of course, as a church gets bigger, and the prospect of a bigger offering appears on the horizon, it's tempting for people in leadership to look first to relatives and close friends to fill key positions in the church. This is why you see churches that hand off the leadership reins to a son or daughter when it's time for the senior pastor to retire or move on.

5. What are the benefits of having significant family involvement in a church, particularly in leadership? What are the dangers? How can a church's leaders make wise, fair decisions about involving family members in their church? Is this even a concern today? Explain.

From the Commentary

> The people were willing to serve Rehoboam if only he would serve them and make life a bit easier for them. All of God's truly great leaders had been servants to the people—Moses, Joshua, Samuel, and especially David—but Solomon had chosen to be a celebrity and not a servant, and Rehoboam was following his bad example. When the Son of God came to earth, He came as a servant (Luke 22:24–27; Phil. 2:1–13), and He taught His disciples to lead by serving.
>
> —*Be Responsible*, page 112

6. What are some ways the king could have served God's people? How did Jesus exemplify service? (See John 13:1–17.) In what ways are we to follow in Jesus' footsteps as we serve others today? (See Matt. 20:25–28.)

From the Commentary

> Let's give Rehoboam credit for asking for a delay to give him time to think and seek counsel. However, time solves

> no problems; it's what leaders *do with time* that really counts. There's no evidence that the king sought the Lord in prayer or that he consulted with the high priest or with a prophet. We get the impression that his mind was already made up but that he was willing to go through the motions in order to please the people. One of the marks of David's leadership was that he was willing to humble himself and seek the mind of God, and then pray for God's blessing on his decisions.
>
> —*Be Responsible*, pages 112–13

7. What happens when leaders spend their time trying to impress people with their skills rather than seeking God? How does this happen in today's church? Where should we turn for spiritual counsel when making important decisions? (See Prov. 11:14; 15:22; 24:6.)

From the Commentary

> The elders gave Rehoboam the best advice: be a servant of the people and the people will serve you. However, Rehoboam had already made up his mind, so he

> immediately rejected that answer and turned to his contemporaries, whom he knew would give him the answer that he wanted. He had no intention of weighing the facts, seeking God's will, and making the wisest choice. In more than fifty years of ministry, I've seen so-called Christian leaders take the Rehoboam approach, do terrible damage to the work of the Lord, and then walk away from the mess, leaving behind poison and debris that will take years to remove.
>
> —*Be Responsible*, page 113

8. What are some ways the ancient world honored age and maturity? Is this still true in today's world? Why or why not? What lessons on choosing leaders can the modern church take from Rehoboam's misguided reign?

More to Consider: Solomon had written a book of practical proverbs about wisdom, one of which said, "A gentle answer turns away wrath, but a harsh word stirs up anger" (Prov. 15:1). How did Rehoboam's leadership contradict what his father had written? In what ways is it obvious that Rehoboam didn't obey Deuteronomy 17:18–20?

From the Commentary

> While Rehoboam was still in Shechem, he attempted some belated diplomacy and sent one of his trusted officers to the assembled ten tribes to try to bring peace or at least keep the discussion going. His choice of mediators was unwise because Adoram [Adoniram] was in charge of the forced labor, and forced labor was one of the irritating areas in the dispute. Perhaps Adoram was authorized to negotiate easier labor arrangements or even lower taxes, but if he was, he failed miserably. The people stoned him, and the frightened king took off for Jerusalem as soon as he heard the news. Rehoboam had followed the wrong counsel, used the wrong approach, and chosen the wrong mediator. What else wrong could he do?
>
> He could declare war!
>
> —*Be Responsible*, page 116

9. How should Rehoboam have responded after he realized he'd listened to the wrong counsel? In what ways was declaring war a way to divert attention from his poor choices? How is this the way some leaders attempt to lead today? Does having a certain power mean you have to use it? Explain.

From the Commentary

> Rehoboam heard and obeyed God's message from Shemaiah, and the Lord began to give him wisdom and bless his life and his work. Had he stayed on that course, he would have led Judah into godliness and true greatness, but he turned from the Lord and lost the blessings he and his people could have enjoyed.
>
> —*Be Responsible*, page 118

10. Review 2 Chronicles 11:5–23. What were some of the ways God began to bless Rehoboam and give him wisdom? Why didn't Rehoboam stay on that course? What led him astray? How can leaders in today's churches avoid falling into this behavior? How can their congregations help them?

Looking Inward

Take a moment to reflect on all that you've explored thus far in this study of 1 Kings 12:1–24; 14:21–31; and 2 Chronicles 10—12. Review your notes and answers and think about how each of these things matters in your life today.

Tips for Small Groups: To get the most out of this section, form pairs or trios and have group members take turns answering these questions. Be honest and as open as you can in this discussion, but most of all, be encouraging and supportive of others. Be sensitive to those who are going through particularly difficult times and don't press for people to speak if they're uncomfortable doing so.

11. Have you ever been passed over for a job or promotion because the boss chose a relative or close friend? Describe the experience and how you felt. How do you deal with unfairness today in the workplace? At church? Even among your family?

12. What are some ways you serve others? How does serving help you grow closer to God? Is serving an easy thing to do? Explain.

13. How do you know whether you're listening to wise counsel or foolish counsel? Describe a time when you listened to foolish counsel. What was the result of that error? What did you learn from that circumstance?

Going Forward

14. Think of one or two things that you have learned that you'd like to work on in the coming week. Remember that this is all about quality, not quantity. It's better to work on one specific area of life and do it well than to work on many and do poorly (or to be so overwhelmed that you simply don't try).

Do you want to pray for discernment and wisdom? Be specific. Go back through 1 Kings 12:1–24; 14:21–31; and 2 Chronicles 10—12 and put a star next to the phrase or verse that is most encouraging to you. Consider memorizing this verse.

Real-Life Application Ideas: Solomon, for all his later failings, was a very wise man. Much of that wisdom is found in the book of Proverbs. This week, go through Proverbs (the entire book or at least a couple of chapters) and copy down wisdom you can make practical use of in your daily life—at work, at home, at church—in all areas where you interact with other people.

Seeking Help

15. Write a prayer below (or simply pray one in silence), inviting God to work on your mind and heart in those areas you've noted in the Going Forward section. Be honest about your desires and fears.

Notes for Small Groups:

- *Look for ways to put into practice the things you wrote in the Going Forward section. Talk with other group members about your ideas and commit to being accountable to one another.*
- *During the coming week, ask the Holy Spirit to continue to reveal truth to you from what you've read and studied.*
- *Before you start the next lesson, read 1 Kings 12:25—14:20; 15—16; and 2 Chronicles 13—16. For more in-depth lesson preparation, read chapters 8 and 9, "A New King, an Old Sin" and "Kings on Parade," in* Be Responsible.

Kings
(1 KINGS 12:25—14:20; 15—16; 2 CHRONICLES 13—16)

Before you begin …

- *Pray for the Holy Spirit to reveal truth and wisdom as you go through this lesson.*
- *Read 1 Kings 12:25—14:20; 15—16; and 2 Chronicles 13—16. This lesson references chapters 8 and 9 in* Be Responsible. *It will be helpful for you to have your Bible and a copy of the commentary available as you work through this lesson.*

Getting Started

From the Commentary

King Jeroboam I was a doer, not a philosopher; he was a man who first caught Solomon's attention because he was busy, efficient, dependable, and productive (1 Kings 11:26–28). He was the ideal popular leader who knew how to fight the people's battles and champion their causes. Ask him about his personal faith in the Lord and his answers might be a bit foggy. He had lived in Egypt

> long enough to develop a tolerance toward idolatry as well as an understanding of how religion can be used to control the people.
>
> —*Be Responsible*, page 127

1. How did Jeroboam use religion to control the people? Read about Nebuchadnezzar in Daniel 3. How did he use religion to control the people? How does this happen even in today's church? What were some of the other serious mistakes Jeroboam made during his reign?

2. Choose one verse or phrase from 1 Kings 12:25—14:20; 15—16; or 2 Chronicles 13—16 that stands out to you. This could be something you're intrigued by, something that makes you uncomfortable, something that puzzles you, something that resonates with you, or just something you want to examine further. Write that here.

Going Deeper

From the Commentary

> Success in life depends on doing God's will and trusting God's promises, but Jeroboam failed in both. When Ahijah gave Jeroboam God's message that guaranteed him the throne of the kingdom of Israel (1 Kings 11:28–39), the prophet made it clear that political division did not permit religious departure. God would have given Jeroboam the entire kingdom except that He had made an everlasting covenant with David to keep one of his descendants on the throne (2 Sam. 7:1–17). This protected the Messianic line so that the Savior could come into the world. The Lord tore the ten tribes away from Rehoboam because Rehoboam had followed Solomon's bad example and turned the people to idols. This should have been a warning to Jeroboam to be faithful to the Lord and stay away from false gods. The Lord also promised to build Jeroboam a "sure house" (a continued dynasty) if he obeyed the Lord and walked in His ways (1 Kings 11:38). What a promise, yet Jeroboam couldn't believe it.
>
> —*Be Responsible*, pages 127–28

3. Review 1 Kings 12:25–33. One of the first evidences of unbelief is fear. How is this evident in Jeroboam's reign? How is this true for us today?

More to Consider: Jeroboam took advantage of the tendency of the Jewish people to turn to idols; and the desire of most people for a religion is that it is convenient, not too costly, and close enough to the authorized faith to be comfortable for the conscience. Jeroboam didn't tell the people to forget Jehovah but to worship Him on the throne of a golden calf close to where they lived. What was so wrong about this decision? In what ways does today's church serve a menu of convenience in worship? What are the risks of making worship all about convenience?

From the Commentary

A religion needs ministers, so Jeroboam appointed all kinds of people to serve as "priests" at the altars in Dan and Bethel (1 Kings 13:33–34; 2 Chron. 11:13–17). The only requirement was that each candidate bring with him a young bull and seven rams (2 Chron. 13:9). God had made it clear when He gave Moses the law that only the sons of Aaron could serve as priests at the altar (Ex. 28:1–5; 29:1–9; 40:12–16) and that if anybody from another tribe tried to serve, he would be put to death (Num. 3:5–10). Even the Levites, who were from the tribe of Levi, were not allowed to serve at the altar on penalty of death (Num. 3:5–10, 38; 4:17–20; 18:1–7). Unauthorized priests at unauthorized temples could never have access to God or present sacrifices acceptable to God. It was a man-made religion that pleased the people, protected the king, and unified the nation—except for the faithful Levites who abandoned the northern kingdom and moved to Judah to worship God according to the teaching of the Scriptures (2 Chron. 11:13–17).

—*Be Responsible*, page 130

4. Why did God install such rigid rules for who could present sacrifices to Him? What greater purpose did that serve? How did Jesus' life, death, and resurrection change all that?

From the Commentary

We live today in an age when "manufactured religion" is popular, approved, and accepted. The blind leaders of the blind assert that we live in a "pluralistic society" and that nobody has the right to claim that only revelation is true and only one way of salvation is correct. Self-appointed "prophets" and ministers put together their own theology and pass it off as the truth. They aren't the least bit interested in what Scripture has to say; instead, they substitute their "feigned [plastic] words" (2 Peter 2:3) for God's unchanging and inspired Word, and many gullible people will fall for their lies and be condemned (2 Peter

> 2:1–2). Jeroboam's "religion" incorporated elements from the law of Moses and from the pagan nations that the Jews had conquered. His system was what is today called "eclectic" (selective) or "syncretic" (combining many parts), but God called it heresy and apostasy. When the prophet Isaiah confronted the new religions in his day, he cried out, "To the law and to the testimony! If they do not speak according to this word, it is because there is no light in them" (Isa. 8:20 NKJV).
>
> Because Jeroboam didn't believe God's promise given by the prophet Ahijah, he began to walk in unbelief and to lead the people into false religion. The religion he invented was comfortable, convenient, and not costly, but it wasn't authorized by the Lord.
>
> —*Be Responsible*, pages 131–32

5. Why is a comfortable religion so appealing? What are some of the comfortable aspects of false religions today? Does there have to be a cost to true religion? Explain.

From the Commentary

> First Kings 13 is not about young and old prophets; it's about King Jeroboam and his sins. The young prophet's ministry is very important in this account, for all that he said and experienced, including his death, were a part of God's warning to King Jeroboam. According to 1 Kings 13:33, the king didn't turn back to God: "After this event Jeroboam did not return from his evil way" (NASB). In this chapter, a prophet died, but in the next chapter, the crown prince died! Obviously, God was trying to get Jeroboam's attention.
>
> —*Be Responsible*, page 132

6. Jeroboam seemed to have an opportunity to change his ways. He even made steps toward that possibility but ultimately turned away from God. What does this path look like for churchgoers today? What is it that ultimately turns people away from seeking God, even if they're initially intrigued by the idea? What are some ways God tries to get nonbelievers' attention today?

From the Commentary

> We don't read in Scripture that Jeroboam sought the Lord's will, prayed for spiritual discernment, or asked the Lord to make him a godly man. He prayed for healing for his arm, and now he asked the prophet Ahijah to heal his son, the crown prince and heir to the throne. It's obvious that physical blessings were more important to him than spiritual blessings. Like many nominal believers and careless church members today, the only time Jeroboam wanted help from God's servant was when he was in trouble.
>
> —*Be Responsible*, page 137

7. Review 1 Kings 14:1–20. How is Jeroboam's convenient cry for help similar to the way so many believers treat God today? Why is it so easy to cry out for help when we're in need and ignore God when we're doing just fine?

From the Commentary

The northern kingdom of Israel had nine dynasties in about 250 years while the southern kingdom faithfully maintained the Davidic dynasty for 350 years, and that was the dynasty from which the Lord Jesus Christ, the Son of David, would come (Matt. 1:1). With all of its faults, the kingdom of Judah was identified with the true and living God, practiced authorized worship in the temple, and had kings who came from David's family. Two of these kings are named in these chapters—Abijah and Asa.

Abijah, son of Rehoboam, was handpicked by his father because of his proven ability (2 Chron. 11:22), but he wasn't a godly man (1 Kings 15:3). He reigned only three years (913–910 BC). He was from David's line through both parents, for David's infamous son Absalom was Abijah's paternal grandfather. Abijah may have had David's blood flowing in his veins, but he didn't have David's strong heart beating in his breast. Abijah's father, Rehoboam, had kept up a running war with Jeroboam, and Abijah carried on the tradition.…

Abijah's son Asa ruled for forty-one years (910–869 BC). He began his reign with a heart like that of David (1 Kings 15:11; 2 Chron. 14:2), but though a good king for most of his life, during the last five years of his reign, he rebelled against the Lord. The word "mother" in 1 Kings 15:10 should be "grandmother," for it refers to the same person

> mentioned in verse 2. The Jewish people didn't identify relatives with the same precision we do today.
>
> —*Be Responsible*, pages 144, 146

8. Review 1 Kings 15 and 2 Chronicles 13—16. What were some of the achievements of Abijah and Asa? What were some of their failures? Why are some kings given tons of attention in Scripture while others are mentioned merely in passing?

More to Consider: Like his father, Asa knew how to call on the Lord in the day of trouble (2 Chron. 13:14–18; 14:11). The king wasn't ignorant of his plight, because he identified Judah as "powerless." Zerah's army was almost twice as large as Asa's, and Asa's men had no chariots. Whether by many soldiers or by few, the Lord could work in mighty power. Asa might have had the words of Jonathan in mind when he prayed that way (1 Sam. 14:6). He might also have been thinking of what Solomon asked in his prayer of dedication (2 Chron. 6:34–35). Sudden deliverance in the midst of battle is a repeated theme in 2 Chronicles (13:14–18; 14:11–12; 18:31; 20:1–30; 32:20–22). Why does God seem to show up "just in time" so often in the Old Testament stories? What does this say about God's timing? How is this different in the New Testament?

From the Commentary

Jeroboam reigned over Israel for twenty-two years (1 Kings 14:20) and became the prime example in Scripture of an evil king (see 15:34; 16:2, 19, 26, etc.). Nadab inherited his father's throne as well as his father's sinful ways. He had reigned only two years when a conspiracy developed that led to King Nadab being assassinated by Baasha, a man from Issachar. Nadab was with the army of Israel, directing the siege of Gibbethon, a Philistine city south of Ekron. This border city had been a source of friction between Israel and the Philistines. It actually belonged to the tribe of Dan (Josh. 19:43–45) and was a Levitical city (Josh. 21:23), and Nadab wanted to reclaim it for Israel.

Baasha not only killed the king, but he also seized his throne and proceeded to fulfill the prophecy of Ahijah that Jeroboam's family would be completely wiped out because of the sins Jeroboam committed (1 Kings 14:10–16). Had Jeroboam obeyed God's Word, he would have enjoyed the blessing and help of the Lord (11:38–39), but because he sinned and caused the nation to sin, the Lord had to judge him and his descendants. That was the end of the dynasty of Jeroboam I.

—*Be Responsible*, page 152

9. In the Old Testament, judgment of one person often led to judgment of that person's entire family and descendants. Why was this the case? Does this mean there was no possibility of grace or forgiveness for the person's descendants? What does this tell us about the way God interacted with His people? What does it tell us about the culture of the time?

From the Commentary

> Baasha set up his palace at Tirzah and reigned over Israel for twenty-four years. Instead of avoiding the sins that brought about the extinction of Jeroboam's family—and he was the man who killed them—Baasha copied the lifestyle of his predecessor! It has well been said that the one thing we learn from history is that we don't learn from history. Baasha had destroyed Jeroboam's dynasty, but he couldn't destroy the word of God. The Lord sent the prophet Jehu to give the king the solemn message that after he died, his family would be exterminated, and another dynasty would be destroyed because of the father's sin. Baasha's descendants would be slain and their corpses become food for the dogs and the vultures.

For a Jew's body not to be buried was a terrible form of humiliation.

Baasha had a normal death, but his son and successor did not. Elah appears to be a dissolute man who would rather get drunk with his friends than serve the Lord and the people. Arza was probably the prime minister. Both men forgot the words of Solomon, who knew a thing or two about kingship: "Woe to you, O land, when your king is a child, and your princes feast in the morning! Blessed are you, O land, when your king is the son of nobles, and your princes feast at the proper time—for strength and not for drunkenness" (Eccl. 10:16–17 NKJV).

The assassin this time was Zimri, the captain of half of the charioteers in the army of Israel. As a noted captain, he had access to the king, and what better time to kill him than when he was drunk? Like Elah's father, Zimri seized the throne, and once he was in power, he killed every member of Baasha's family.

—*Be Responsible*, pages 152–53

10. Baasha had fulfilled the prophecy of Abijah, and Zimri had fulfilled the prophecy of Jehu. Does this mean they were innocent of their crimes? Why or why not? How did the Lord hold them accountable?

Looking Inward

Take a moment to reflect on all that you've explored thus far in this study of 1 Kings 12:25—14:20; 15—16; and 2 Chronicles 13—16. Review your notes and answers and think about how each of these things matters in your life today.

Tips for Small Groups: To get the most out of this section, form pairs or trios and have group members take turns answering these questions. Be honest and as open as you can in this discussion, but most of all, be encouraging and supportive of others. Be sensitive to those who are going through particularly difficult times and don't press for people to speak if they're uncomfortable doing so.

11. Have you ever felt manipulated by a religious leader? Describe that circumstance. What was the leader's purpose behind the manipulation? How can you discern when someone is trying to manipulate you rather than sincerely teach or direct you?

12. Describe a time when you struggled with belief. What role did fear play in that season of life? How did you find your way back to believing? Or if

you're still struggling, what obstacles are keeping you from faith and how can you overcome them?

13. Have you ever been judged because of something a family member did? How was this similar to the way people were often judged in Old Testament times? What is an appropriate, godly response to being judged unfairly?

Going Forward

14. Think of one or two things that you have learned that you'd like to work on in the coming week. Remember that this is all about quality, not quantity. It's better to work on one specific area of life and do it well than to work on many and do poorly (or to be so overwhelmed that you simply don't try).

Do you want to take a step away from fear and toward trust in the Lord? Be specific. Go back through 1 Kings 12:25—14:20; 15—16; and 2 Chronicles 13—16 and put a star next to the phrase or verse that is most encouraging to you. Consider memorizing this verse.

Real-Life Application Ideas: The Israelites didn't always have great leaders. Many of them were quite awful. Take time this week to honor the best leaders in your life. Take a pastor or other leader out for lunch or coffee and use that opportunity to celebrate his or her role in your life. Do something nice for your boss at work. Call someone who mentored you in the past. Look for simple, small ways to say thank you to the leaders who have had a positive impact on your life.

Seeking Help

15. Write a prayer below (or simply pray one in silence), inviting God to work on your mind and heart in those areas you've noted in the Going Forward section. Be honest about your desires and fears.

Notes for Small Groups:

- *Look for ways to put into practice the things you wrote in the Going Forward section. Talk with other group members about your ideas and commit to being accountable to one another.*
- *During the coming week, ask the Holy Spirit to continue to reveal truth to you from what you've read and studied.*
- *Before you start the next lesson, read 1 Kings 17—19. For more in-depth lesson preparation, read chapters 10 and 11, "Let the Fire Fall!" and "The Cave Man," in* Be Responsible.

The Cave
(1 KINGS 17—19)

Before you begin …

- *Pray for the Holy Spirit to reveal truth and wisdom as you go through this lesson.*
- *Read 1 Kings 17—19. This lesson references chapters 10 and 11 in* Be Responsible. *It will be helpful for you to have your Bible and a copy of the commentary available as you work through this lesson.*

Getting Started

From the Commentary

Elijah the Tishbite suddenly appears on the scene and then leaves as quickly as he came, only to reappear three years later to challenge the priests of Baal. His name means "The Lord (Jehovah) is my God," an apt name for a man who called the people back to the worship of Jehovah (1 Kings 18:21, 39). Wicked King Ahab had permitted his wife Jezebel to bring the worship of Baal into Israel (16:31–33), and she was determined to wipe out the worship of Jehovah (18:4). Baal was the Phoenician fertility god who sent rain and bountiful crops, and the rites connected with his worship were unspeakably immoral. Like Solomon who catered to the idolatrous practices of his heathen wives (11:1–8), Ahab yielded to Jezebel's desires and even built her a private temple where she could worship Baal (16:32–33). Her plan was to exterminate the worshippers of Jehovah and have all the people of Israel serving Baal.

—*Be Responsible*, page 157

1. Why was Ahab swayed by Jezebel? Why were so many people intent on exterminating the worshippers of Jehovah? What did they fear?

More to Consider: Read Malachi 4:5–6; Matthew 17:3, 10–13; Luke 1:17; and John 1:19–23. What do these verses tell us about the importance of the prophet Elijah? What is it about Elijah's story that makes him a significant character in the New Testament?

2. Choose one verse or phrase from 1 Kings 17—19 that stands out to you. This could be something you're intrigued by, something that makes you uncomfortable, something that puzzles you, something that resonates with you, or just something you want to examine further. Write that here.

Going Deeper

From the Commentary

> The Jewish people depended on the seasonal rains for the success of their crops. If the Lord didn't send the early rain in October and November and the latter rain in March and April, there would soon be a famine in the land. But the blessing of the semiannual rains depended on the people obeying the covenant of the Lord (Deut. 11). God warned the people that their disobedience would turn the heavens into bronze and the earth into iron (Deut. 28:23–24; see Lev. 26:3–4, 18–19). The land belonged to the Lord, and if the people defiled the land with their sinful idols, the Lord wouldn't bless them.
>
> It's likely that Elijah appeared before King Ahab in October, about the time the early rains should have begun. There had been no rain for six months, from April

to October, and the prophet announced that there would be no rain for the next three years! The people were following Baal, not Jehovah, and the Lord could not send the promised rain and still be faithful to His covenant. God always keeps His covenant, whether to bless the people for their obedience or to discipline them for their sins.

God had held back the rain because of the fervent prayers of Elijah, and He would send the rain again in response to His servant's intercession (James 5:17–18). For the next three years, the word of Elijah would control the weather in Israel!

—*Be Responsible*, page 158

3. Why did the blessing of the semiannual rains depend on the people obeying the covenant of the Lord (Deut. 11)? Why would God give Elijah the power to control the weather? What does this say about the relationship between God and Elijah? Between God and His people?

From the Commentary

> After Elijah left the king's presence, Jezebel must have instigated her campaign to wipe out the prophets of the Lord (1 Kings 18:4). As the drought continued and famine hit the land, Ahab began his search for Elijah, the man he thought caused all the trouble (18:17). In one sense, Elijah did cause the drought, but it was the sins of Ahab and Jezebel that led the nation into disobeying God's covenant and inviting His chastening. The Lord had a special hiding place for His servant by a brook east of the Jordan, and He also had some unusual "servants" prepared to feed him. The Lord usually leads His faithful people a step at a time as they tune their hearts to His Word. God didn't give Elijah a three-year schedule to follow. Instead, He directed His servant at each critical juncture in his journey, and Elijah obeyed by faith.
>
> "Go, hide yourself!" was God's command, and three years later the command would be, "Go, show yourself!"
>
> —*Be Responsible*, page 159

4. How did Elijah's three-year absence create a spiritual drought in the land? In what ways was Elijah's silence a judgment from God? (See Ps. 74:9.)

From the Commentary

> Elijah lived at Cherith [Kerith] probably a year, and then God told him to leave. God's instructions may have shocked the prophet, for the Lord commanded him to travel northeast about a hundred miles to the Phoenician city of Zarephath. God was sending Elijah into Gentile territory, and since Zarephath was not too far from Jezebel's home city of Sidon, he would be living in enemy territory! Even more, he was instructed to live with a widow whom God had selected to care for him, and widows were usually among the neediest people in the land. Since Phoenicia depended on Israel for much of its food supply (1 Kings 5:9; Acts 12:20), food wouldn't be too plentiful there.
>
> —*Be Responsible*, page 160

5. Why might it be significant that God sent Elijah into Gentile territory? What was the point of sending him into a place where there was probably suffering and need? What does this tell us about trusting God's plans?

From the Commentary

> First Kings 17:17–24 is the first recorded instance in Scripture of the resurrection of a dead person. The evidence seems clear that the widow's son actually died and didn't just faint or go into a temporary swoon. He stopped breathing (v. 17), and his spirit left the body (vv. 21–22). According to James 2:26, when the spirit leaves a body, the person is dead. The great distress of both the mother and the prophet would suggest that the boy was dead, and both of them used the word "slay" with reference to the event (1 Kings 17:18, 20).
>
> —*Be Responsible*, page 162

6. Review 1 Kings 17:17–24. What was the mother's response to her son's death? How are her words similar to the disciples' question in John 9:2? What was Elijah's response? What did it take for the Lord to raise the boy from the dead? What is significant about the number three here?

From the Commentary

> If Elijah could have described to a counselor how he felt and what he thought, the counselor would have diagnosed his condition as a textbook case of burnout. Elijah was physically exhausted and had lost his appetite. He was depressed about himself and his work and was being controlled more and more by self-pity. "I only am left!" Instead of turning to others for help, he isolated himself and—worst of all—he wanted to die. (Elijah never did die. He was taken to heaven in a chariot. See 2 Kings 2.) The prophet concluded that he had failed in his mission and decided it was time to quit. But the Lord didn't see it that way. He always looks beyond our changing moods and impetuous prayers, and He pities us the way parents pity their discouraged children (Ps. 103:13–14). First Kings 19 shows us how tenderly and patiently God deals with us when we're in the depths of despair and feel like giving up.
>
> —*Be Responsible*, pages 173–74

7. How does 1 Kings 19 begin? Why did the prophet argue with the Lord and try to defend himself? What was the ultimate result of his disagreement with God? What were the messages he was responding to?

From the Commentary

> When the torrential rain began to fall, Jezebel was in Jezreel and may have thought that Baal the storm god had triumphed on Mount Carmel. However, when Ahab arrived home, he told her a much different story. Ahab was a weak man, but he should have stood with Elijah and honored the Lord who had so dramatically demonstrated His power. But Ahab had to live with Queen Jezebel, and without her support, he knew he was nothing. If ever there was a strong-willed ruler with a gift for doing evil, it was Jezebel. Neither Ahab nor Jezebel accepted the clear evidence given on Mount Carmel that Jehovah was the only true and living God. Instead of repenting and calling the nation back to serving the Lord, Jezebel declared war on Jehovah and His faithful servant Elijah, and Ahab allowed her to do it.
>
> —*Be Responsible*, page 174

8. Review 1 Kings 19:1–4. Why did Jezebel send a messenger to Elijah when she could have sent soldiers and had him killed? How might Jezebel's plans have been foiled if she had transformed the prophet into a martyr? How did God ultimately deal with Jezebel's plans?

From the Commentary

> When the heart is heavy and the mind and body are weary, sometimes the best remedy is sleep—just take a nap! Referring to Mark 6:31, Vance Havner used to say that if we didn't come apart and rest, we'd come apart—and Elijah was about to come apart. Nothing seems right when you're exhausted.
>
> But while the prophet was asleep, the Lord sent an angel to care for his needs. In both Hebrew and Greek, the word translated "angel" also means "messenger," so some have concluded that this helpful visitor was another traveler whom the Lord brought to Elijah's side just at the right time. However, in 1 Kings 19:7, the visitor is called "the angel of the Lord," an Old Testament title for the second person of the Godhead, Jesus Christ, the Son of God.
>
> —*Be Responsible*, page 177

9. Read Genesis 16:10; Exodus 3:1–4; and Judges 2:1–4. How is the way the angel of the Lord spoke and acted in these passages similar to the way he spoke to Elijah in 1 Kings 19:5–8? What does this tell us about God's relationship with Elijah?

More to Consider: It was about two hundred miles from Beersheba to Sinai (Horeb), a journey of perhaps ten days to two weeks. It had been three weeks at the most since Elijah fled from Jezreel, but the trip expanded to consume forty days (1 Kings 19:8)! If Elijah was in such a hurry to put miles between himself and Jezebel's executioners, why did he take such a long time to do it? Consider Moses' journey in Exodus 34:28. Elijah had to deal with Baal worship, and Moses had to deal with the worship of the golden calf (Ex. 32). Why did Elijah make a cave his home? How is this similar to modern-day spiritual retreats?

From the Commentary

Elijah had nothing new to say to the Lord, but the Lord had a new message of hope for His frustrated servant. The Lord had many reasons for rejecting His servant and leaving him to die in the cave, but He didn't take that approach. "He has not dealt with us according to our sins, nor punished us according to our iniquities.... For He knows our frame; He remembers that we are dust" (Ps. 103:10, 14 NKJV).

First, the Lord told Elijah to return to the place of duty. When we're out of the Lord's will, we have to retrace our steps and make a new beginning (Gen. 13:3; 35:1–3).... But Elijah was called to serve, and there were tasks to perform. When Joshua was brokenhearted because of Israel's defeat at Ai, he spent a day on his face before God, but God's answer was, "Get up! Why do you lie thus on your face?" (Josh. 7:10 NKJV). When Samuel mourned over the

> failure of Saul, God rebuked him. "How long will you mourn for Saul, seeing I have rejected him from reigning over Israel? Fill your horn with oil, and go" (1 Sam. 16:1 NKJV), and Samuel went and anointed David to be the next king.
>
> —*Be Responsible*, pages 182–83

10. Review 1 Kings 19:15–21. In what ways was Elijah having a "pity party" during this time of his life? What was God's main message to the hiding man? How is this message relevant to believers today?

Looking Inward

Take a moment to reflect on all that you've explored thus far in this study of 1 Kings 17—19. Review your notes and answers and think about how each of these things matters in your life today.

Tips for Small Groups: To get the most out of this section, form pairs or trios and have group members take turns answering these questions. Be honest and as open as you can in this discussion, but most of all, be encouraging and supportive of others. Be sensitive to those who are going through particularly difficult times and don't press for people to speak if they're uncomfortable doing so.

11. Think of a time when someone influenced your choices in a negative way. Why were you swayed when you knew better? What does it take to stand strong in your beliefs when others are challenging them? Where do you turn to get that strength?

12. Describe a time when you felt totally burned out. How did that come about? What did that burnout do to your relationship with God? What are some practical ways to avoid getting to that point?

13. Describe a time when you felt like running away to a cave. What prompted that feeling? What was your faith like during that season? How did you find your way out of that self-pity?

Going Forward

14. Think of one or two things that you have learned that you'd like to work on in the coming week. Remember that this is all about quality, not quantity. It's better to work on one specific area of life and do it well than to work on many and do poorly (or to be so overwhelmed that you simply don't try).

Do you want to turn to God about something instead of giving in to self-pity? Be specific. Go back through 1 Kings 17—19 and put a star next to the phrase or verse that is most encouraging to you. Consider memorizing this verse.

Real-Life Application Ideas: As soon as you can schedule it, take a retreat to reconnect with God and rest in His Word. This isn't a time to run away from God, but to sit quietly in His presence. Perhaps your church has a retreat you can participate in, or maybe you can simply get away on your own or with a few close friends. Turn off all the noise of the electronic age, and spend the time away in a quieter place where God can speak to you and refresh your tired spirit.

Seeking Help

15. Write a prayer below (or simply pray one in silence), inviting God to work on your mind and heart in those areas you've noted in the Going Forward section. Be honest about your desires and fears.

Notes for Small Groups:

- *Look for ways to put into practice the things you wrote in the Going Forward section. Talk with other group members about your ideas and commit to being accountable to one another.*
- *During the coming week, ask the Holy Spirit to continue to reveal truth to you from what you've read and studied.*
- *Before you start the next lesson, read 1 Kings 20—22. For more in-depth lesson preparation, read chapters 12 and 13, "Ahab, the Slave of Sin" and "Reflections on Responsibility," in* Be Responsible.

Ahab

(1 KINGS 20—22)

Before you begin …

- *Pray for the Holy Spirit to reveal truth and wisdom as you go through this lesson.*
- *Read 1 Kings 20—22. This lesson references chapters 12 and 13 in* Be Responsible. *It will be helpful for you to have your Bible and a copy of the commentary available as you work through this lesson.*

Getting Started

From the Commentary

In his novel *Moby Dick*, Herman Melville gave the name Ahab to the deranged captain of the whaling vessel *Pequod*. (Melville also included a "prophet" named Elijah.) The Ahab in the Bible is a weak man who destroyed himself and his family because he allowed his evil wife, Jezebel, to turn him into a monster. The name Jezebel is familiar to people today and has even made it into the dictionary: "Jezebel—an evil, shameless woman." To call a woman

> "a Jezebel" is to put her on the lowest level of society (see Rev. 2:20–23). The prophet Elijah described the man accurately when he told Ahab, "I have found you, because you have sold yourself to do evil in the sight of the Lord" (1 Kings 21:20 NKJV).
>
> First Kings 20—22 describes four events in Ahab's life: three battles with the Syrians (Aram) and a land-grab scam that involved an illegal trial and several murders.
>
> —*Be Responsible*, page 189

1. What were some of the ways Ahab was enslaved to sin? What do we learn about God in the story of Ahab and his wife? What do we learn about ourselves?

2. Choose one verse or phrase from 1 Kings 20—22 that stands out to you. This could be something you're intrigued by, something that makes you uncomfortable, something that puzzles you, something that resonates with you, or just something you want to examine further. Write that here.

Going Deeper

From the Commentary

> First Kings 20:1–30 records the first of two occasions when wicked King Ahab showed a glimmer of spiritual understanding. Israel was just coming out of three years of famine when Ben-hadad, King of Syria, decided to attack and take advantage of their plight. King David had defeated these northern nations (called Syria in the older translations, Aram in the newer ones), but these nations had gradually regained their independence. Another factor in Ben-hadad's attack was the growing strength of Assyria in the north. Ben-hadad wanted to control the trade routes through Israel because he had lost the northern routes to Assyria, and he also wanted to be sure that Israel would provide men and weapons in case of an Assyrian invasion.
>
> —*Be Responsible*, page 190

3. What was Ahab's glimmer of spiritual understanding? How is his character similar to those of misguided leaders in today's world? What are the dangers of a leader having a glimmer of spiritual understanding?

More to Consider: The thirty-two "kings" who allied with Ben-hadad were the rulers of northern city-states whose safety and prosperity depended a good deal on the strength of Syria. We aren't told how long the siege of Samaria lasted, but Syria ultimately brought Ahab to the place of submission. First, Ben-hadad demanded Ahab's wealth and family, and Ahab agreed. Ben-hadad planned to hold the family hostage just to make sure Ahab didn't back out of his agreement. Why didn't Ahab call for Elijah or another prophet to help? Why did he capitulate? Contrast this choice with Saul's decision in 1 Samuel 11.

From the Commentary

> In opposing Ben-hadad, Ahab had nothing to stand on, but God in His grace sent him a message of hope: The Lord would give Ahab the victory.… As He did on Mount Carmel, so Jehovah would do on the battlefield.…
>
> Following the example of Solomon (1 Kings 4:7ff.), Ahab's father, Omri, had divided the kingdom of Israel into a number of political districts, each in the charge of a "provincial leader" who was also an army officer. The Lord selected these leaders to lead the attack against Syria, and Ahab was to lead the small army of 7,000 men. They went out at noon, knowing that Ben-hadad and his officers would be eating and drinking and be in no condition to fight a battle. Even when Ben-hadad's scouts reported that a company of men was approaching the Syrian camp, the Syrian king wasn't afraid but told the guard to take them alive. The military strategy for capturing prisoners

> would be different from that for destroying an invading army, so Ahab's men caught the Syrian guards by surprise and proceeded to wipe out the Syrian army. Instead of measuring the dust of Samaria as he threatened (20:10), Ben-hadad jumped on his horse and escaped with his life.
>
> —*Be Responsible*, page 191

4. Why did God choose to send a message of hope to a man who was obviously not following Him? How was this an opportunity for God to demonstrate that He alone was God (1 Kings 18:36–37)? Why did God give Ahab a victory here?

From the Commentary

> When God sent King Saul to fight the Amalekites, He made it clear that He wanted the Israelites to completely destroy them (1 Sam. 15). Saul disobeyed the Lord and as a result lost his kingdom. The Lord must have given a similar command to King Ahab (1 Kings 20:42), but he, too, disobeyed. Ahab won the battle but lost the victory. What the enemy couldn't accomplish with their weapons,

> they accomplished with their deception. If Satan can't succeed as the lion who devours (1 Peter 5:8), he will come as a serpent who deceives (2 Cor. 11:3). Even Joshua fell into a similar trap (Josh. 9).
>
> —*Be Responsible*, page 192

5. Review 1 Kings 20:31–43. In what ways did Ahab lose the victory? Does this seem fair, given that Ahab was being merciful? How did God confront Ahab after the battle? Who were the "sons of the prophets"? (See 2 Kings 2:3–7; 4:38–40.)

From the Commentary

> Ben-hadad was the man Ahab should have killed, but he set him free, and Naboth was the man Ahab should have protected, but Ahab killed him! When you sell yourself to do evil, you call evil good and good evil, light darkness and darkness light (Isa. 5:20). The infamous episode of Naboth's vineyard reveals the lawlessness of King Ahab and his evil wife, Jezebel. Consider the sins they

> committed and consequently the commandments of God that they disdained and disobeyed.
>
> —*Be Responsible*, page 194

6. Review 1 Kings 21:1–16. How did Ahab and Jezebel commit each of the following sins: idolatry, covetousness, false witness, murder, and stealing? Why would God allow such a duo to rule? What does this teach us about how God can use evil people to further His kingdom?

From the Commentary

> "Surely the Lord God does nothing, unless He reveals His secret to His servants the prophets" (Amos 3:7 NKJV). We have heard nothing from or about Elijah since he called Elisha to be his successor, but now God brings His servant into center stage to confront the king. As He always does when He gives an assignment, He told Elijah just what to say to the evil king. Ahab had shed innocent blood and his guilty blood would be licked up by the dogs. What a way for the king of Israel to end his reign!

> Previously, Ahab called Elijah "the troubler of Israel" (1 Kings 18:17 NKJV), but now he makes it more personal and calls the prophet "my enemy." Actually, by fighting against the Lord, Ahab was his own enemy and brought upon himself the sentence that Elijah pronounced. Ahab would die dishonorably and the dogs would lick his blood. Jezebel would die and be eaten by the dogs. All of their posterity would eventually be eradicated from the land. They had enjoyed their years of sinful pleasure and selfish pursuits, but it would all end in judgment.
>
> —*Be Responsible*, pages 197–98

7. What was Ahab's response to Elijah's confrontation? What was God's response to that? Later events proved that Ahab's repentance was short-lived, but the Lord at least gave him another opportunity to turn from sin and obey the Word. Why wasn't Ahab easily convinced? In what ways did Ahab's marriage to Jezebel make it a foregone conclusion that he would choose sin over following the Lord?

From the Commentary

At this point we are introduced to godly Jehoshaphat, king of Judah. A summary of his reign is found in 1 Kings 22:41–50 and even more fully in 2 Chronicles 17—20. He followed in the way of David and sought to please the Lord (17:1–6). He sent teaching priests throughout the land to explain God's law to the people (vv. 7–9) and assigned the other priests to serve as faithful judges to whom the people could bring their disputes. God gave Judah peace, and Jehoshaphat took advantage of this opportunity to fortify the land (vv. 10–19).

He was a good king and a godly leader, but he got involved in three costly compromises. The first was the "bride compromise" when he married his son to a daughter of Ahab and Jezebel (2 Chron. 18:1; 21:4–7; 1 Kings 22:44; 2 Kings 8:16–19). This led to the "battle compromise," when Jehoshaphat got entangled in affairs of his son's father-in-law when Syria attacked Israel (2 Chron. 18:2—19:3). Ahab's evil influence affected the reign of Jehoshaphat's grandson Ahaziah (2 Chron. 22:1–9), and the "battle compromise" almost cost Jehoshaphat his life (1 Kings 22:32–33). The third compromise was the "boat compromise," when Jehoshaphat foolishly joined forces with Ahab's son Ahaziah (1 Kings 22:48–49; 2 Chron. 20:31–37) and tried to get rich by importing foreign goods. The Lord wrecked his fleet and rebuked him for his sinful alliance.

—*Be Responsible*, pages 198–99

8. Review 1 Kings 22 and 2 Chronicles 18. Why did Jehoshaphat make these compromises? What does this teach us about the temptations good leaders face? What leads godly leaders to make poor decisions?

More to Consider: The name Jehoshaphat means "whom God judges," that is, "God pleads His cause." Why is this a particularly appropriate name for him? What were his greatest accomplishments?

From the Commentary

> Micaiah was under a great deal of pressure to agree with the false prophets and assure Ahab he would defeat Syria. Not only was Micaiah outnumbered four hundred to one, but the officer who brought him to the two kings also warned him to agree with the majority. Often in Scripture, it's the *minority* that's in the will of God, and Micaiah was determined to be faithful, not popular. The sight of the two kings on their thrones, dressed in their royal robes, must have been impressive, but it didn't sway Micaiah.
>
> —*Be Responsible*, page 200

9. Review 1 Kings 22:13–23. What was Ahab's response to Micaiah's message? Was it an honest response? Explain.

From the Commentary

A nation, a church, a family, or an individual is never so far gone that the Lord can't give a new beginning. Elijah was Ahab's enemy because Ahab was following his own agenda and not the Lord's. Elijah was God's servant and risked his life to bring the nation back to the God of Abraham, Isaac, and Jacob. True reformation should lead to spiritual renewal. It isn't enough to tear down the pagan altars and remove the priests of Baal. We must rebuild the Lord's altar and ask God for new fire from heaven to consume the sacrifices.

Reformation means getting rid of the accretions of the new things to get back to the foundations of the old things. When Israel abandoned her covenant with Jehovah, she ceased to be the people of God and became like the other nations. The beautiful temple that once housed the glory of God became a pile of ruins that bore witness to the sins of an ungrateful and unbelieving people. God's chosen

> people forgot their glorious past and deliberately manufactured a future that brought shame and ruin.
>
> —*Be Responsible*, page 211

10. What role does the struggle between true prophets and false prophets play in a nation's faith? In what ways do the false prophets tell us what we want to hear? How is that different from what we need to hear?

Looking Inward

Take a moment to reflect on all that you've explored thus far in this study of 1 Kings 20—22. Review your notes and answers and think about how each of these things matters in your life today.

> *Tips for Small Groups: To get the most out of this section, form pairs or trios and have group members take turns answering these questions. Be honest and as open as you can in this discussion, but most of all, be encouraging and supportive of others. Be sensitive to those who are going through particularly difficult times and don't press for people to speak if they're uncomfortable doing so.*

11. Have you ever worked for a leader like Ahab? Without naming names, describe that situation. What was it like to work for someone who had evil intent? What is a godly response to a leader who is going directly against what you believe?

12. Describe a time when someone confronted you because of some sin or wrongdoing in your life. How did that make you feel? In what ways was it necessary? Have you ever confronted someone because of his or her sin? How did you go about it?

13. What is your experience with false prophets or leaders? Have you ever been tempted to follow someone who later turned out to be a fraud? What led you to follow that person? How did you discover the person wasn't preaching the true gospel message?

Going Forward

14. Think of one or two things that you have learned that you'd like to work on in the coming week. Remember that this is all about quality, not quantity. It's better to work on one specific area of life and do it well than to work on many and do poorly (or to be so overwhelmed that you simply don't try).

Do you want to confront a leader who is in sin? Be specific. Go back through 1 Kings 20—22 and put a star next to the phrase or verse that is most encouraging to you. Consider memorizing this verse.

Real-Life Application Ideas: Much of the Old Testament story is about God reminding His people of their past so they can make the right choices in their present. This week, spend time reviewing your personal faith history. Consider the key moments in your journey and how they have brought you to this place, today. Then thank God for all the twists and turns, because each of them was important in making you the person you are today.

Seeking Help

15. Write a prayer below (or simply pray one in silence), inviting God to work on your mind and heart in those areas you've noted in the Going Forward section. Be honest about your desires and fears.

Notes for Small Groups:

- *Look for ways to put into practice the things you wrote in the Going Forward section. Talk with other group members about your ideas and commit to being accountable to one another.*
- *During the coming week, ask the Holy Spirit to continue to reveal truth to you from what you've read and studied.*

Summary and Review

Notes for Small Groups: This session is a summary and review of this book. Because of that, it is shorter than the previous lessons. If you are using this in a small-group setting, consider combining this lesson with a time of fellowship or a shared meal.

Before you begin …

- *Pray for the Holy Spirit to reveal truth and wisdom as you go through this lesson.*
- *Briefly review the notes you made in the previous sessions. You will refer back to previous sections throughout this bonus lesson.*

Looking Back

1. Over the past eight lessons, you've examined 1 Kings (and parts of 1 and 2 Chronicles). What expectations did you bring to this study? In what ways were those expectations met?

2. What is the most significant personal discovery you've made from this study?

3. What surprised you most about 1 Kings? What, if anything, troubled you?

Progress Report

4. Take a few moments to review the Going Forward sections of the previous lessons. How would you rate your progress for each of the things you chose to work on? What adjustments, if any, do you need to make to continue on the path toward spiritual maturity?

5. In what ways have you grown closer to Christ during this study? Take a moment to celebrate those things. Then think of areas where you feel you still need to grow and note those here. Make plans to revisit this study in a few weeks to review your growing faith.

Things to Pray About

6. First Kings is a book about responsibility. As you reflect on what it means to be responsible with your faith, seek God's wisdom and guidance for how you can live a life of consistent and intentional faith.

7. The messages in 1 Kings include faithfulness, responsibility, hope, trust, and God's presence. Spend time praying for each of these topics.

8. Whether you've been studying this in a small group or on your own, there are many other Christians working through the very same issues you discovered when examining 1 Kings. Take time to pray for them, that God would reveal truth, that the Holy Spirit would guide you, and that each person might grow in spiritual maturity according to God's will.

A Blessing of Encouragement

Studying the Bible is one of the best ways to learn how to be more like Christ. Thanks for taking this step. In closing, let this blessing precede you and follow you into the next week while you continue to marinate in God's Word:

May God light your path to greater understanding as you review the truths found in 1 Kings and consider how they can help you grow closer to Christ.